THE ART OF
SILHOUETTE

THE MUSICIAN: By EDOUART.

(In the possession of A. B. Connor, Esq.)

THE ART OF SILHOUETTE

BY DESMOND COKE

LONDON : MARTIN SECKER
NUMBER FIVE JOHN STREET ADELPHI

BY THE SAME AUTHOR

HELENA BRETT'S CAREER
THE BENDING OF A TWIG

ETC.

First published 1913

PRINTED AT
THE BALLANTYNE PRESS
LONDON

CONTENTS

		PAGE
	WARNINGS—AND ADVERTISEMENT	11
I.	IN PRAISE OF COLLECTING	17
II.	A DEFENCE OF SHADOWS	29
III.	THE MEN BEHIND THE SHEET	41
IV.	DECADENCE	71
V.	EDOUART	97
VI.	CUPID AND SILHOUETTE	121
VII.	LABELS	135
VIII.	SOME COLLECTIONS	159
IX.	" CUT PAPER "	181
X.	PRACTICAL	205
XI.	NOW—AND WHAT THEN ?	217
	INDEX	

PLATES

Facing p.

    I. The Musician, by Edouart   *Frontispiece*

   II. A Lady, by Charles   22

  III. Two Beaux, by Charles and Miers   24

  IV. The Austere Art of Silhouette   30

   V. The Soft Charm of Silhouette   36

  VI. Two Ladies, by Mrs. Beetham   48

 VII. A Lady, by Mrs. Beetham   50

VIII. A Pair, by Rosenberg   54

  IX. Silhouette in Red, by Spornberg   58

   X. A Lady, by Miers, Leeds   62

  XI. Silhouette Jewels   66

 XII. A Royal Pair, assigned to Charles   72

XIII. Gold-tinted Silhouette, by Hervé   76

XIV. The Girl with the Bonnet, by Frith   78

 XV. Two Young Bucks, by Hubard and Gapp   80

XVI. The Sisters, by Beaumont   84

XVII. A Victorian Young Lady   90

XVIII. An Undergraduate, by Edouart   98

XIX. A Famous Actor, by Edouart   102

 XX. A Family, by Edouart   108

XXI. A Group, by Torond   112

XXII. A Silhouette Hand Screen   114

PLATES

Facing p.

XXIII. A Page from Edouart's Folios 118

XXIV. A Family, by Adolphe 122

XXV. A Group, by Laura Mackenzie 128

XXVI. A Lady, by Mrs. Beetham 136

XXVII. Framed Miniatures, by Miers and Beetham 142

XXVIII. A Family, assigned to Field 146

XXIX. The Spinet-Player, by Torond 148

XXX. A Pope and a Soldier, by Foster 160

XXXI. William Pitt, by Fepk 166

XXXII. A Red-Coat Officer 170

XXXIII. A Calligraphic Silhouette 174

XXXIV. A Negative Silhouette 176

XXXV. A Memorial Design 182

XXXVI. Heraldic Emblem 188

XXXVII. The White Houses 192

XXXVIII. The Angler's Repast 200

XXXIX. An Officer, by H. P. Roberts 210

XL. A Modern Specimen, by Phil May 218

XLI. Cuttings by Hubard and Edouart 222

IN LOVE
TO MY MOTHER
WHO GAVE ME—AMONG MUCH ELSE—
THE FIERCE JOY OF COLLECTING

"*Un même penchant nous unit*"

WARNINGS—AND ADVERTISEMENT

THIS is a book, not a tome.

It is intended, not for historians, antiquaries, experts, or curators : but rather for collectors, artists, lovers of the past, general readers, and all who think nothing human or curious alien from themselves.

It is not a History of Silhouette. A work properly so named has lately been produced by Mrs. Nevill Jackson, who has traced her subject with scholarly completeness, fully analyzed the various processes, and added an exhaustive alphabetic list of all known profilists, however humble.

This is a lighter book, which dares to think that silhouettes are not a very solemn subject, albeit once referred to by a back-street dealer as "them funeral things." The pleasures of collecting, what one can still find well worth collecting, the best-known profilists who worked in England, their curious labels, the bond of Love with Silhouette all down the ages, some vindication of a gentle art too long

11

misunderstood—these form only a few ingredients in the salad of my book.

There will be no pompous, satisfying " we " ; no ancient tales of so-called silhouettes upon Etruscan vases, familiar in a dozen articles from magazines, nor much (I hope) on Étienne de Silhouette ; and I shall not pursue my subject through France, Germany, and Russia to the pale-eyed East. In spite of this I trust that there is not a little information boiled down from my note-books for these pages. I have not wantonly let anything of interest slip.

In any case, however others like it, I have written this book from a real love of my subject and have loved writing it. Fourteen years have passed since, a Freshman of Oxford, I fared out into the High Street and, feeling somewhat reckless, paid eighteen-pence for two full-length profiles by Edouart. . . . I have been buying ever since, although alas ! at annually increasing prices. These essays therefore represent the fourteen-year experience of a mono-maniac who claims to be among the earliest of his peculiar brand.

There are mistakes of course. As to this I can only say that gratitude shall leaven the grief with which I receive corrections.

WARNINGS

It is futile, no less than ungracious, for second-comers to depreciate the pioneers, nor am I likely to wrong in such a way my good friend Mrs. Nevill Jackson, who has done everything within her power to help me in the chapter upon Edouart. It is in justice only to myself, should any critic find the same passages quoted in us both, that I here say the notes on which this book is based were largely made before the "History" was published or indeed begun. Any resemblance is therefore due to a mere common source. I have read Mrs. Jackson's book with interest and profit, then put it aside and tried to see how differently I could write my own. There is enough in Silhouette to fill a dozen volumes (I have touched only on the profilists who worked in England), and I hope these two first may be regarded as supplementary to one another.

As to the pictures, it is neither pardonable love nor yet a sinful pride which has ordained that they should largely be from specimens in my possession ; but mere utility. Had my aim been to fill these pages with The Best Silhouettes, I should have canvassed all collectors for their specimens by Miers, Charles, and Mrs. Beetham. It seemed, however, much more useful to show, instead, each of the many methods used and at the least one silhouette by all of the most famous artists : a guide by which owners might set a name to their pet specimens. This I have kept before me in my buyings and my sellings (for the collector must do both), so that I believe the specimens here reproduced give a fair idea of each profilist at his best and most typical. That is, at least, their aim.

Enough ! One word, brief but no less sincere, of thanks must first be given to Mrs. Nevill Jackson, the Lady Sackville, and Mr. Francis Wellesley for their generous help, as also to all the collectors whose names will be found in these pages. Then, ignoring the contempt of those superior people mentioned in my second line, and with one last kindly warning to all who think that such a book as this should hold a purple patch or two on dainty Lady Betty, with the word " vastly " as refrain, let us take unashamed our pleasure in the old-world puppet show and, leaving cleverness to others, chat easily about the shadows that we love.

I
IN PRAISE OF
COLLECTING

CHAPTER I

IN PRAISE OF COLLECTING

THE collector is usually thought a crank by his acquaintance, a nuisance by his friends, a miser by his relatives, a blessing by the dealers, and a deluded idiot by every one concerned. He is, as a matter of fact, the happiest—if the poorest—of God's creatures. He is the poorest, because if some miraculous twist of the wheel made him a millionaire to-morrow, he would merely collect white elephants instead of silhouettes and never have the cash to pay for all of them. . . . But he is the happiest, because he is obeying Nature's law.

The wise Aristotle, in beginning his great work upon the Life Political, laid it down that Man is a social creature, but forgot to state that he is also a collecting animal. From the earliest dawn of history and long before it, he has obeyed one instinct, the instinct to amass. The cave man, as we know, collected flints (I hope my history is right)—or wives. Adam probably came home, some days, delighted with a specially fine fig-leaf. Eve possibly collected apples, which would explain a lot. Drive out Nature with a pitchfork, said the Roman poet, she will hurry back. You cannot stop Man from collecting. All the world seeks something : curios, stamps, sovereigns, or adventures. The man-made law has ruled out scalps and wives, but other things remain. As long as it allows the curio-shops to open even five and a half days out of the seven, so long will Man find a way to gratify the universal instinct.

What lies beneath it ? Dangerous to ask, of anything ; but I expect it has been long ago established that the collecting mania, like any form of sport, is based deep down upon a natural vanity. The cricketer thrusts forward fitness as his god, the connoisseur declares that he walks fifteen miles a day and walking is the *real* way to get fit : but one in his own hidden soul takes pride to hit a ball when others would have missed, a second is delighted to detect a forgery or recognize from well across a road the shops where they are always selling off, with an all-day electric light casting its glamour on their " antique " jewels.

Equally Man needs excitement ; an old truth which explains things so diverse as football, juvenile crime, and collecting. Life, left to itself, sends along its thrills too slowly ; but the collector, if always destitute of funds, never can lack expectation. Each day he fares out along the shops (for he will drift to London and soon learn half a hundred different productive routes), sure every day that fate will send him one of those historic finds that stand like milestones in the History of Art: a crystal ewer sold as glass or at the least a Raeburn for five shillings. And when instead he only finds a print or silhouette at probably one-quarter of the West-end price, with what joy does he bear it back—collectors are the only men who carry parcels along Piccadilly ;—with what excited hands unwrap it, safely home ; with what delirious haste find a small space for it upon his crowded walls ; how often leave his work and ramble absently, to find himself before his latest treasure ! Each day is too short for him. He is never lonely, and can not be bored. He is the favourite of fortune.

I have known people who collected spurs, corks, potted-meat lids, bobbins, pistols, playbills, labels from decanters, imperfect books, siege money, peasants' rings, insurance plates, illustrated music covers, suppressed plates, forgeries, masonic emblems, knockers, buttons, shoes, and Indian basketry. I have heard of a man who collected visiting cards, with the tiny pasteboard of Tom Thumb as his especial gem ; another who spent his lifetime seeking the twelfth Delft plate to complete his set, and found the owner of it finally to be a man whose sole remark was, "How much do you want for your eleven ?" . . and I have read about another rich collector, who bought single copies of first-edition Dickens' till he had got a set, when he sold, caring little what they fetched, and so began his blissful hunt again. All these men, pitied by their friends, were happy, for they had found an interest in life and rose each day with a new hope. Health, business, family— the world in these ways might be terribly unkind ; but who could ever tell ? Perhaps that very afternoon fortune would throw across their path the perfect potted-meat lid or the ideal bobbin ! And life becomes a splendour to the man who has eternal hope for even a small thing.

At first, of course, one buys at random anything. This seems cheap, that is early, the other is only a very little cracked. . . . Later, however, one begins to realize two facts. Only a billionaire could hope to make a good collection of everything antique, and the man who wishes bargains must know more than any given dealer. Hence grows that modern malady, specialization; for each collector wishes in the end to be the owner of a great collection, and not too far below the surface of all Britons there is lurking Shylock. The young collector sells his early purchases, burns the forgeries that are his connoisseur wild oats, and fixes on a subject.

And yet—and yet who can resist a bargain? The medley on my walls accuses me, though long enough ago I vowed to specialize in Silhouette.

Certainly the man who keep himself for even a few years to one particular collection—reading articles upon it, asking prices, seeing the specimens of others, above all constantly upon the hunt—has his reward as slowly he begins to realize that dealers are curiously ignorant. That is how the truth comes home at first, for he does not reflect that the poor dealer must know something about everything, whilst he—he has specialized and, never knowing it, he has become an expert!

Perhaps this narrow way rules out those big adventures at which I have hinted, but who shall say that humble connoisseurs are not rewarded with their little thrills? yes, and their little tragedies.

Oddly enough, the name of Charles brings back an episode in either kind from my adventures in the strait field of Silhouette.

The first at Oxford, a dozen years ago. The back-street dealer, selling me a fine brass oval frame for a few shillings, rubs the grimy surface of its glass with finger scarcely whiter and remarks: " There's something in it, too, sir. It's dirt cheap at that." Imagine if, still full of youth's romance, I snatched it eagerly out of his hands, refused all wrapping, and hugged the new find with especial fervour as I rushed straight back to my College rooms. Even so soon, I knew that graceful oval beaten out of brass as the most early sort of Silhouette frame. . . . And when, sacrificing a new handkerchief, I cleaned the dirt of ages from its glass, there lay beneath it the superb example of Charles' genius which graces plate ii of the present volume !

Sometimes I amuse myself, in abstract mood, with the debate : should I have returned it to the dealer, had he not obviously sold the picture also by his last remark? Ruskin, I think, somewhere has debated a like question, but I forget his answer. Mine generally is, No. The dealer takes his chance : the buyer is allowed his luck. Knowledge ought to be

PAINTED IN BLACK & GREY ON CARD

By Charles.

its own reward. Nor would any conscience money taken to a dealer reach the poor owner who sold it to *him*.

The other episode bound up with this graceful painter of the shadow portrait has only half a happy ending. The scene a Sussex farm; the period, lately. Upon one side of a dresser the delightful portrait seen upon plate iii; upon the other a similar wood oval frame, a like decorated glass, but void of silhouette. Tommy (I feel sure that would be his name), "a most mischievous boy," one day some years ago had come into the parlour and "rubbed the likeness off." . . . With misdirected gallantry he had begun upon the lady. Looking at the beau, imagine the belle's languor, her banked hair, her dainty laces, the tilt of her proud chin but the redeeming softness of her smile! Oh, Tommy, Tommy, where, I often wonder, are you now? Are you perhaps an artist, penitent? or more deservedly in Wormwood Scrubs? . . . Perhaps it may console all but the kid-glove sentimentalists to learn that Tommy, embarking on the last half of his work, was found and given a good caning. The other frame is not in my collection. It would have been too grim, like the chair empty at a Christmas feast.

It is a popular fallacy that the collector must be a rich man. As a matter of contrary fact, it has been shown already that if he is worth his salt, he never has a penny ! But sophistry apart, the real collector has no need for any special income. He spends no more upon his hobby than other men on theirs, whether they be horses, wine, or taxis. He simply must adjust the choice of subject to his means. You can't be too poor to collect ; you easily may be too rich. What fun in collecting if once you can afford to buy in the most costly market; if once the thrill of a find vanishes, the dare-devil sensation of I Oughtn't But I Must ? No, what the ideal collector needs is knowledge ; knowledge and a little pluck. He must not lean on signatures or pedigrees, for these are what cost money. He must discover for himself and not pay bigger prices for another's finds. He must shake free from the worship of names, and mistrust all that is written on a work of art—except in the technique itself, for every one with eyes to read. Lastly, he must perhaps " be not the first by whom the new is tried," for nobody may follow, but even less " the last to lay the old aside." Like a cunning journalist, he must read signs and portents in the public taste, buying not what every one is

Plate III.

TWO BEAUX

Painted (1) on glass by Charles, and (2) on chalk by Miers, London.

iii

II

A DEFENCE
OF SHADOWS

CHAPTER II

A DEFENCE OF SHADOWS

COLLECTORS in general, notwithstanding all of the above, have always been a race for whom there is reserved a special brand of genial enough pity, as for lunatics essentially harmless; and Silhouette in particular has exacted martyrdom in all ages of its devotees, as witness the tragic episode of Edouart set forth upon a later page.

Thus I do not complain when, asked at a dinner-party what I specially collect, my answer draws the comment: "Oh, how interesting, yes! *I* know. Those little cut-out things. They did them on the piers." . . . I do not complain of this. I am long hardened. But it inspired this chapter.

The first thing to be said is that a silhouette is not, as many imagine, any form of a daguerreotype. The silhouette-collector's scorn for this last production is kin to that of the old-master expert for a silhouette. We can never understand at all each other's vices!

29

The next thing to be said, and later to be proved, is that it is not necessarily cut from paper. True, some of the earliest profiles were so produced ; true, many artists give most praise to those severe black heads with their fully adequate austerity (plate iv); but connoisseurs have long ago agreed that Miers, Mrs. Beetham, Rosenberg, and Charles are a quartette supreme in that hey-day of silhouette, the eighteenth century. Now all these, it will presently be shown, painted their portraits, whether on card, glass or plaster, and (save for such variations from type as three early-cut Beethams I have recently unearthed) never relapsed on the cut-paper method, which they doubtless loftily despised.

The best silhouettists never touched a pair of scissors.

There ! I have set it on a line apart, and in italics like a serial's climax. Were I but Sterne, or did I live in a day when publishers were tame, it should be on a page apart, with vast black lines around and red hands pointing index fingers at the little central lump of type. For there lies Silhouette's whole vindication, and through the ignorance of it have many insults long been piled upon a very charming, nor too easy, art.

These old-time profiles, miniature paintings not

THE AUSTERE ART OF SILHOUETTE

(1) Cut by Mrs. Beetham. (2) Mrs. John Lewes.
(3) "Shelley." (4) Hollow-cut silhouette.

a half-crown cut-out, were not taken—equally—
on piers. The galleries of the great profilists were
cheek by jowl with the great artists' studios, at
quite impeccable addresses, nor did a lower class by
any means consort to them. Frankly in snobbish
vein, since men will do much for their enthusiasms,
I set down at random a list of great folk who have
not despised to hold traffic with the profilist. First
of all, George III, who seems to have spent half his
reign posed against white screens ; Queen Charlotte,
naturally involved with him, though she was also a
collector on her own account ; Princess Elizabeth,
their child, herself a profilist of merit ; Mrs. Delaney,
of course ; Mrs. Fitzherbert, with her own private
gallery ; Perdita Robinson, faithless for a moment
to the painters; George IV, to whom G. Atkinson
of Brighton boasts to be " sole profilist " ; William
IV and even Queen Victoria, who sat to Master
Hubard ; Napoleon, giving profiles—it is said—
as souvenirs; Nelson (but beware of forgers); Pitt,
more than once, and Fox ; Goethe, who loved the
art and practised it no less, as perfect specimens on
Mr. Wellesley's wall attest ; Gibbon, protruberant
with snuff-box, for a frontispiece ; Goldsmith (now
in the National Portrait Gallery); Mrs. Leigh Hunt,

herself a cutter of great merit, as shown by portraits of Byron and Keats ; Sir Walter Scott, who sat to Edouart at Edinburgh in 1831 ; Paganini, by the same, as also the exiled Charles X, who sat to him at Holyrood ; or later still, Browning by Master Hubard —these with Wellington, Fanny Burney, Burns (who sat to Miers : see the Clarinda Correspondence, January and February 1788), the Pompadour, and countless duchesses must surely touch the souls of such as think nothing of an art till it is patronized by the nobility.

Or if there be those, and certainly there are, who value works of art by nothing but the prices paid, they may thrust from their mind the vision of a full-length portrait cut in black and framed complete for half a crown, if they will concentrate on dainty and expensive . . . miniatures superbly painted under a fine glass of gold and white ; glorious specimens of black and gold on glass ; priceless china, brooches, jewelled rings ; or—gem of Mrs. Nevill Jackson's beautiful collection — an ivory patch-box, gold-mounted and with two panels of superb enamel flanking a wee portrait signed by Miers. None of these things cost little when first made, and they have not gone down in value.

Again, for each man has his own peculiar god, if it be that authority is needed, let it here be said that the galleries and museums, tardily awakened, are buying specimens at last, whilst the Victoria and Albert has lately given space to a fine loan collection.

But those who have once learnt the charm of this ancient and delightful art will seek for a more pleasant sanction. They may find it in a German author of 1780, quoted in a twenty-year-old article by Andrew Tuer, who probably can claim to be the pioneer in Silhouette's revival so far as penmen go. "This art," writes this ingenious German, "is older than any other. In Arcadie itself profiles were drawn. The shepherds of that golden age, in their happy simplicity, traced shadows of their beloved on the sand—to worship in absence. . . ." And later he says, though less nicely: "But now again, since this new culture, profiles are asked for since they give a truer idea of the face than the daubs of the ignorant. The taste of Man has revolted against Affectation and gone back to the Simple."

The new culture was of course Lavater's science, physiognomy, and Lavater himself is no less glowing in his praise of profiles. "What more imperfect," he exclaims, "than a portrait of the human figure drawn after the shade ! And yet what truth does not this portrait possess ! This spring, so scanty, is for that reason the more pure. . . ." Lavater builds his whole system largely upon silhouettes, of which in the quarto edition he gives some beautiful examples, and not content with this, hints at "a separate Work" wherein to treat of their significance more fully. "He that despises shades," says he, "despises physiognomy;" or, in more ecstatic vein, he refers to Silhouette as "Little gold but the purest," a slender art but eloquent.

Ruskin, another giant for such as worship names (I slowly spread my net, unseen), says in *Præterita :* "I had always been content enough with my front face in the glass, and had never thought of contriving vision of the profile. The cameo finished I saw at a glance to be well cut, but the image it gave of me was not to my mind. I did not analyze its elements at the time, but should now describe it as a George the Third's penny, with a halfpenny-worth of George the Fourth, the pride of Amurath the Fifth, and the temper of eight little Lucifers in a swept-lodging."

This confession from a connoisseur of beauty

does much to justify Lavater in his praise of shadows.

The fact is that we moderns, always excepting those who join the theatrical profession, have come to dread the sight of our own profiles. We are like Ruskin, "content enough" with our front face, and it is this view that the photographer decides to take after a swift tactful side-glance at our chins and noses. In the days before it was considered dowdy for a woman to show more than her lips from underneath her hat, in the good old days when languid beauties posed on elbow-cushions the better to turn coldly an exact profile on their importunate admirers, it was expected of these last also that they should have their silhouettes taken for the lady's pleasure. And she, no doubt, pored over the learned Lavater's plates, trying to see which passion dominated her intended. . . . All this perished with photography. We can go right through life "content enough" with our full-face, giving our inner self away to every one but our complacent selves.

These things ought not so to be. It is every man's plain duty to see his profile once. . . .

Photography indeed, the chinless mortal's refuge, threatens to play him false, for in its most artistic form it long ago relapsed largely upon silhouette-effects and now its popular exponents are hastily seeing, with white screens and flashlights behind, what profit can be got from this revival of the shadow-portrait.

To defend Silhouette from the heavy standpoint of those who claim it as a document would be mere cruelty, an insult to a most dainty art. Perhaps no Gainsborough or Lely, with flattering brush, could throw the light on old coiffures that may be gained from eight early silhouette prints of dressed heads that lie in my portfolio ; probably no better record of the first authentic Peeler could be found than that quaintly hatted policeman who hangs upon the wall at Knole ; certainly no portrait would be so pitiless in its revelation to a female mind of " the hang of the skirt " in the eighteenth-century costume as two full-length profiles, a rarity so early, showing the coiffure and contour in an inimitable manner. But these advantages, if such they be, are mere side-issues to the connoisseur, who cares for none of them.

No, if he had to justify the silhouette, he would soar to far loftier heights, to Plato maybe and his image of the Cave. Perverting that great philosopher's

THE SOFT CHARM OF SILHOUETTE

1. By Mrs. Bull.
2. Eda O., 1799-1819.
3. G. A. Girling, by Lane Kelfe.
4. A Lady, unknown.

idea of a man chained within a prison, seeing all men and things that passed as shadows thrown against the light and knowing them as outlines only, he might build up a fine theory as to the reality of shadows alone in a world where colour has been proved a luxury added by each of us to that vague Thing Itself. . . .

Luckily there is a simpler way. Izaac Walton, having written immortally on fishing, added these equally undying words : " And next let me add this, that he that likes not the book should like the excellent picture of the trout, and some of the other fish." So I ; or in the equally fine words of another great man, " Si monumentum requiris, circumspice." If you like not my pleading on behalf of shadows, you should like the exquisite fineness of the profiles by Mrs. Beetham, the dignity of Rosenberg, the character of Edouart, the convincing pleasantness of those simpler portraits that I have massed on one page and might call after a scrapbook formula, "Four Favourites " (pl. v). If you seek Silhouette's best praise, merely turn these pages. Looking on those dainty miniatures or chiselled outlines, artistry superb in either case, the just man no longer will judge Silhouette by the cheap specimens poured forth

for these last fifty years from the arcades and piers, to which photography too long has banished its defeated rival.

Absurd that these crude outlines, snipped for six coppers and received with giggles, should any longer be allowed to prejudice the judgment upon Mrs. Beetham ! Nobody thinks the less of Cosway because dear modern ladies persist in painting miniatures, nor do we posthumously condemn Gainsborough because he was a Royal Academician. . . .

The whirligig of time truly brings in its revenges, and there are some who hope that the camera, which has killed so much that was beautiful, from wood-engraving downward, may yet see the West-end, its one-time temple, again triumphantly invaded by its ancestral foe, Nature's own real art, the shadow.

III

THE MEN BEHIND
THE SHEET

CHAPTER III

THE MEN BEHIND THE SHEET

THE mystic-sounding title to this chapter is largely allegorical, for there is little reason to suppose that all the profilists here named actually used a sheet, or anything approaching it, whilst practising their art.

There is a familiar eighteenth-century print, from Lavater's quarto edition, that clearly shows what may be best described as the sheet method of taking likenesses in shade. This is entitled " A Sure and Convenient Machine for Drawing Silhouettes." Upon the left, half hidden by his square sheet (paper, need I add ?), stands the artist, totally absorbed ; centre, as actors say, sits a lady of the period, so intent upon looking her best that in an agony she clutches with both hands the posts and stays which hold the artist's sheet firm to her chair ; and to the right a candle on elaborate carved stand, to lend a touch of dignity no doubt to the whole studio.

A French variant differs only in the candle's greater luminosity and in the head-dress of the lady, who has abandoned the English *négligé* of loose hair for an elaborate coiffure. Above the English print and underneath the French occurs this diagnosis of the sitter by Lavater : " This is the Character I would assign to the silhouette of this Young person ; I find in it, Goodness without much Ingenuity, Clearness of Idea, and a ready Conception, a mind very industrious, but, little governed by a lively Imagination, and not attached to a rigid punctuality ; we do not discern in the Copy, the Character of Gaiety which is conspicuous in the Original ; but the Nose is improved in the silhouette, it expresses more Ingenuity. . . ." Face-experts have never won the name for gallantry ; nor would it seem (to be no less unsparing) that aptitude in punctuation always goes with skill in physiognomy.

A less-known print of slightly later period, entitled simply " Method of Taking Profiles," clearly owes its origin equally to whichever version of the other was first in the field : for though the two protagonists are lavishly redressed, their positions reversed, and the candle given a more homely table, the chair is copied slavishly, the man stands as before, the lady still clutches at the post and stay. This artist clearly did not wish to alter anything that possibly could spoil a process probably unknown to him by anything except his copy. Candle-stand and dress were safe : but we may fancy him reflecting, this poor nervous plagiarist, that if the lady let go of that stay, it might mean wrecking the whole silhouette. . . .

Our own knowledge, unhappily, is not much superior, for though there are advertisements of sundry wonderful machines, which are considered elsewhere in this volume, there is (so far as I can learn) no way of discovering whether Rosenberg, for instance, actually used any such contrivance or whether, like most modern silhouettists, he scorned even the sheet method and trusted to his eyes and a white background only. These mechanic chairs and general abracadabra methods would appeal, I imagine, only to so-called " Papyrotomists " and not to any artist proper.

Lavater, however, was more concerned with actuality than art ; he valued profiles only as the most exact of portraits : and so is found giving the most elaborate instructions to those who wish to take a person's shade, but at the same time (be it noted) in such a way as to make it clear that his apparatus was not in ordinary use.

" The common method," he distinctly says (vol. ii.

chapter vii., 1789 octavo edition), " is accompanied
with many inconveniences. It is hardly possible the
person drawn should sit sufficiently still; the
designer is obliged to change his place, he must ap-
proach so near to the person that motion is almost
inevitable, and the designer is in the most inconvenient position; neither are the preparatory steps
everywhere possible, nor simple enough."

Here, in this passage written at the heyday of shade-
taking, is the undoubted *locus classicus*, as pedants
say, or stock passage for the " common method ";
and it seems to me that, with its cryptic last three
words, it lays itself open to just about as many con-
tradictory and utterly convincing explanations as any
table of statistics or debated scripture. Here, at any
rate, is what Lavater liked :

" A seat purposely contrived would be more convenient. The shade should be taken on post paper,
or rather on thin oiled paper, well dried. Let the
head and back be supported by a chair, and the shade
fall on the oil paper behind a clear, flat, polished glass.
Let the drawer sit behind the glass, holding the frame
with his left hand, and, having a sharp blacklead
pencil, draw with the right. The glass, in a detached
sliding frame " (grimly, be it added, like the business

part of a guillotine), " may be raised or lowered, according to the height of the person. The bottom of the glass frame, being thin, will be best of iron, and should be raised so as to rest steadily upon the shoulder. In the centre, upon the glass, should be a small piece of wood or iron, to which fasten a small round cushion, supported by a short pin, scarcely half an inch long, which, also, may be raised, or lowered, and against which the person drawn may lean. By the aid of a magnifying lens, or solar microscope, the outlines may be much more accurately determined and drawn."

If this be " simple " by comparison, the common method must indeed have been a nightmare ; but at the risk of seeming obstinate, I will not, until proof arrives, believe that artists like Miers, Rosenberg, or Mrs. Beetham, who claimed to rank with the great miniaturists of their period, fastened their sitters into a chair so reminiscent of the dentist's parlour or expected them to look pleasant with the iron entering into their shoulder. . . .

In any case, the artist is his work, nor can his methods have any interest beyond the technical. Of the great profilists it may be said, that when the shadow had been duly traced, their labours had not yet begun. A child or an automaton could do so much—and both, as we shall see, were doing it ere half a century had passed. The life-sized shade must first of all be brought down to prettier dimensions —later, at any rate, by a machine, whatever these first artists did—and then began the infinitely delicate work which formed the artist's individual hall-mark.

How individual, only a connoisseur or any one observant beyond the usual can judge. Even with those who used the scissors only, there is no confusion possible ; an Edouart is as different from a Gapp as, say, a Cosway from an Engleheart. Swift who so soon as 1745 has more than one verse on the lady's new accomplishment, remarks about Clarissa's shade of a man, cleverly enough adorned with a " grey worsted stocking " eye :

> " *I must confess that as to me, sirs,*
> *Though I ne'er saw her hold the scissars,*
> *I now could safely swear it is her's.*"

This being so, it has seemed to me worth while to give a short description of the most characteristic points in the work done by the best profilists. Many silhouettes, " Family " or collected, are unsigned ;

still more bear the wrong artists' names piously inscribed upon their back ; and it will be easy for any one, using these notes and the accompanying plates, to remedy these things, which most assuredly ought not so to be.

Place aux dames! Indeed—as often—they deserve it.

To Mrs. Beetham must be awarded the palm of merit among profilists, unless the judge be anyone whose tastes run to a classic sternness. She, as befits her sex, had nothing of that quality. Hers not to leave Nature's own shade in its uncompromising, beautiful simplicity : she held the mirror up and lo ! her sitters found themselves (one almost must suspect) more graceful, delicate and fair than even they themselves had hitherto suspected. No bow is out of place ; no ribbon lies in any but a perfect curve ; no single hair strays save where it is almost fatally becoming ; no one could be more beautiful— until you see the next.

Examine Miss Di Jones and Mrs. Mathews, who face each other on plate vi, just as they were taken together, in Fleet Street, during the month of July 1792.

The faces, as in all of Mrs. Beetham's shades, are

left most properly in a dead black ; her art is given its full rein with ribbons, jewels, hair and dress. Beneath a microscope (and surely that is how she must have looked at them whilst working) each hair, one can literally state, may be separately seen. Before work which combines so rarely the wonder of absolute detail and the charm of general effect it is hard indeed to refrain from the modern weakness of superlatives : impossible for even the fruitiest conservative to hold back from poor Silhouette, so long rejected and misunderstood, the grand old name of " Art "—defamed by every music hall and soiled with all ignoble use.

By no means every specimen retains its labels—the dear Victorians have seen to that—and some have even lost their frames : but I believe, till somebody corrects me, that I have discovered a sure and easy test for Mrs. Beetham's work in her odd convention for finishing the bust. Most profilists cut off the body with a natural curve, but Mrs. Beetham seems always to have made it end in a way which reference to the illustrations on plate vi, vii, or xxvi will make clearer than two chapters of description. Rosenberg had somewhat the same trick, but those who turn to plate viii will find it different enough to be easily distinguished.

MISS DI JONES & MRS. MATHEWS

Painted on glass by Mrs. Beetham, July, 1792.

vi.

No one, in any case, could fail to recognize the touch of Mrs. Beetham. She is the very luxury of Silhouette. The woman's hand is there, delicate, fine : and when, as with our ladies here, the Beetham decoration is around the portraits—firm white and gold design, with more erratic spots inside—there can be no mistake. Fine, dignified, old oval frames in dark brown pear-wood lend the last touch to a perfect decoration (plate vii). *page. 50.*

Yet not the last, for Mrs. Beetham's best work is painted on a convex glass ; behind, there is a slab of chalk ; and thus Miss Di Jones throws her charming profile, much as she did in the flesh more than a century ago, dead black upon the white behind. That Mrs. Mathews, on the right side of my mantel-piece, can not do quite the same is merely a price exacted by the laws of light and a mania for " pairs."

Charles, of the same period and 130 Strand, " opposite the Lyceum," was another London pro-filist who literally made shadow-pictures. Neither artist kept to the one formula ; no doubt some clients found the cream and gold glass too costly, so that one finds both working on mere humble card, whilst Charles upon his labels describes himself as

" the original inventor on glass." Upon the other hand, both painted also miniatures on ivory (for which Charles asked four guineas), and on plate xxvii may be found a nice specimen of Mrs. Beetham in this—to me—less satisfying mood. No, having once seen their real shadow-pictures, one feels inclined, as urged by the advertisement, to refuse utterly All Other Kinds ! Charles' young dandy flings forward on the chalk his bored, contemptuous shade in a manner which, alas, is better not even attempted by photography. (Plate iii.) *page 24.*

Charles was niggardly with labels, and unless specimens are signed minutely below the bust or on it (as with the last specimen) his hair-work is the safest clue. Charles painted hair by an ingenious formula combining an apparent minuteness with rapidity of execution. At a first glance his detail seems no less astonishing than that of Mrs. Beetham ; but look again and you will see that where that careful lady conscientiously painted each hair of every separate lock, the easy-going male, with a hand cynically free, left on the paper a swift tangle, giving hardly less of an effect. It must not, indeed, be supposed by any ardent partisan in the fast-spreading sex-war that we have here a patent indication of the female's superior

Plate VII

SHADOW-PORTRAIT ON GLASS

By Mrs. Beetham, 1795.

(In the possession of Francis Wellesley, Esq.)

thoroughness ; for Charles was an artist (was he not R.A. ?) and as such quite willing to give labour where it repaid its time. A glance at the beau's cravat or ruffle will establish this.

It may be said of Charles, more even than of other profilists, that he must be astounded, and at times disgusted, if from the other plane he can observe the many silhouettes in various collections that bear the name of Charles. . . . It seems, in fact, enough that any specimen on card should be of the late eighteenth century : " by Charles " appears forthwith upon its back, without so much as that small " ? ", which might allow a second trial hereafter in an age less ignorant of Silhouette. The work in particular of Mrs. Bull (plate v), another clever woman-profilist, ~~page 36.~~ who worked " Opposite the India House " around 1785, is seldom signed and almost exactly similar in style to that of Charles : a serious problem for those anxious intelligently to put " attributions " upon their collection.

Rosenberg is possibly the easiest quarry for those engaged in this most fascinating sport. Let it be said at once that in this, as in all else, rules are a mere stumbling-block to those who light first on the exceptions : each of the great profilists experimented upon methods other than his own ; but at his most typical, Rosenberg of Bath is almost unmistakable, even if he had been less lavish with his labels. Painted for the most part on flat glass, of an uncompromising hardness which (we shall see, when labels are examined) he intended " in imitation of stone," encased generally in a square brass frame with oval opening, his portraits could never be confused with those of anybody unless Jorden. He is the most severe of profile-painters, and such curious aberrations as the blue sash across a George IV in Mr. Wellesley's collection must be accounted the exception. Colour, usually, rules out Rosenberg.

Luckily, however, further proofs are still forthcoming. Every collector worthy of the name wastes hours in every day trifling with his pet specimens : and once, unframing a fine Rosenberg—with no very special object beyond the pleasure of reframing it— I hit upon a very interesting fact. The black bust had always seemed to be against a background of white paper ; but now in one hand I held a black profile upon glass and in the other a pink profile on white paper !

Immediately four other Rosenbergs must be unframed—an excellent excuse for yet more waste of time—and although bought from various sources all of them showed the same backing.

Rosenberg, in fact, set his stern black outlines against a bright pink background ; perhaps, I think, with some idea of gaining an effect of marble ; and this pink silhouette, left where the black-painted glass has defied the colour-eating sun, is no less sure a proof of Rosenberg's work than a label for those who find it behind their specimens.   Incidentally they will come on a generous layer of antique paper, scribbled over with brush-marks and pencil lines ; even, if so lucky as myself, some little memory of the artist himself. On one such pencilled sheet appears this fragment of methodical direction :

> Mrs. Richard . . .
>> No. 8 Georg . . .
>>> before 4.

Rosenberg, it has been said, usually worked with the black mass, an authentic shadow, and his weakest portraits are those in which he tried to indicate a ruffle or the wave of hair.   The inconclusive thin brown-looking outline that results is curious in so fine a craftsman.   For this reason he is more successful, as a rule, with his male portraits.   The method of

Charles or Mrs. Beetham suited Woman and her dainty laces better than the hard outline of Rosenberg or Edouart. The Bath beau who tilts his chin superbly on plate viii would be even better, robbed of his quite inconclusive ruffle.

If this be not enough for those who think they may possess a Rosenberg, here is another hint. Mr. Weymer Mills, in one of those dainty articles of his which waft one back magically to the gay and charming period of Silhouette, remarks : " On the back of each Rosenberg portrait, scarcely decipherable, is that magic word Bath." I must, however, add for the benefit of those whom this discourages, that long and ardently as I have peered at the back of my seven specimens (five of them with labels) I never yet have come upon the magic word.

For those who find a fascination in this sport of attribution, a sport at which some amateurs are all too skilful, Spornberg might seem a godsend but in reality is just the opposite. He is, in an expressive phrase, Too Easy. There is no sport at all. A Spornberg silhouette is literally " signed all over."

Spornberg, for line or elegance, is not to be compared with the other great profilists who worked in England at his period, the late eighteenth century.

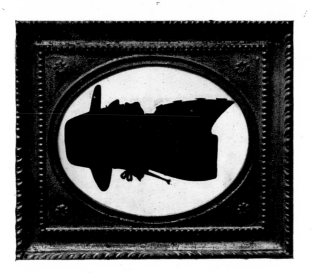

PAINTED ON GLASS BY ROSENBERG.

(Labelled : in original Rosenberg frames).

viii.

There is a certain lack of definition, a fluffiness, about his portraits, and a careless handling of costume detracts not a little from the faces, which are life-like enough. He probably would never have won any reputation except for his originality of process. Spornberg may be said to have adapted on glass the earliest form of paper-silhouette—the " hollow-cut "—and to have added a refinement. He painted in black upon the inside of convex glass the hollow outline, as it were, of his sitter's profile, so that the glass was all opaque and black except for a white profile. On this white portion he roughly painted, still in black, hair, eye, ear, even lines or wrinkles, with just a few brush-splutters that might be said to stand for gown or coat. The portrait was now done. Spornberg or an assistant now scraped an elaborate, although crude, oval pattern round the portrait and next applied red pigment lavishly behind, till portrait and border alike stood out bright red against the sombre black.

Messy perhaps the method, and dubious the art of its result : but none the less, set in its fine gilt oval, a startlingly rich whole and a delightful decoration, holding its own as such with almost any form of silhouette.

Spornberg, in whom neatness cannot ever have

been the prime virtue, scratched a crude signature before the red paint was applied. These inscriptions vary between " W. Spornberg invenit Bath," and " W. Spornberg fecit Bath," as well as in the absence or presence of a date. Lady Sackville at Knole has no fewer than eight Spornbergs of the Ansley family, dated from 1773 to twenty years later. Two in my collection (pl. ix), gems with an added value as a gift of friendship, are both signed "W. Spornberg fecit Bath " (except that neither of the t's is crossed), but only upon the male portrait is the date set, "1793." To one of those at Knole we are indebted for the knowledge of his workshop, 5 Lower Church Street, Bath. In a day when every other building bears its mural tablet, "Here lived So-and-So," it would be worth while to commemorate in stone the places where great men and fair ladies thronged to have their portraits taken by this "new and fashionable " art, now dead.

Strictly, no doubt, Foster of Derby should rank with the next century : but as he is said to have lived from 1761 to 1864, there is some latitude in time. Dates are the chief obstacle to anyone who would explore a subject so long neglected and indeed despised as Silhouette : and I have not been able to

56

discover exactly in what year Foster started work. A
portrait by him of Pope Pius VI in 1799 (pl. xxx) may ~Page160.~
have been among his earliest achievements (Foster
in that year would be 38), or may have been merely
copied from Marchant's relief of the Pope published
as an engraving by Colnaghi in the early months of
the next year. In any case, whatever his century,
the fact that he worked in red brings him conveniently
on the scene here. Foster's red, however, pales into a
brown by Spornberg's, and is relieved with gold. Mrs.
Nevill Jackson thinks it probable that Foster used a
machine for taking the outline itself (that record
which a profilist would need who advertised, as most,
"Original shades kept"), but be this as it may, his
work upon that outline was both elaborate and good.
The face alone, in this case, is of a dark russet brown,
the hair and costume gold ; whilst on one specially fine
specimen presented to me by a kind dealer-friend, the
subject, besides the glory of a gold dress spattered
with minute gilt trefoil pattern, bears the adornment of
a gold hat trimmed splendidly in white and green.
This pattern on his ladies' dresses is indeed a kind of
Foster hall-mark. Another specimen, this time in
the rarer blue-grey, bears the same design—minute
spots grouped in threes—but gracefully enough in

white : for this is a Foster that lacks gold. The portrait of Pope Pius VI has the papal insignia (I choose a word at random) blazoned on its coat in gold. Three men, two soldiers and a seeming undergraduate, are done no less in red and gold, but each has an effective touch of black up at his neck.

Foster was either not quite fortunate about his sitters or else he exaggerated noses—a thought which makes me doubt yet more his use of that machine— but for the rest he gained a marvellous effect of life. The perky soldier on plate xxx is always picked out as a splendid study by those who suffer my collection, knowing nothing about Silhouette and clutching gladly at a human topic. " Can't you *see* him ? " they exclaim. . . . And so indeed you can : the rakish angle of his cap, the pouted chest, the half-smile on his lips—dear me, to think that he lived long before America had given us the great word, swank ! . . . Well, he avoided rag-time, and I hope that Life was kind to him, as he deserved. He cheers me up and is a friend of mine.

Foster, to my mind, has not been given his due place among the greater profilists. Perhaps his actual originality, his groping after a new form, counted as nothing but a vice to people that knew

PAINTED IN RED ON GLASS

By Spornberg : Bath, 1793.

not the Grafton Galleries. Foster is the very Post-Impressionist of Silhouette. He was not satisfied with the old order and its limitations: he wanted freedom, demanded to get nearer Nature; but (it is here the parallel must fail) he seldom lost sight of the beautiful. Perhaps the fact that he discarded labels for the most part, signing underneath the bust, may be a proof that he considered himself artist and not showman. In any case he proved himself something of an epicure in frames. The typical brass-oval of a Foster papier mâché frame must have been a luxury of cost, for it is good both in design and workmanship; but those who have experimented know well the difference made in even the best silhouette by any change of setting—and Foster above all things was an experimentalist. Some of his frames, in place of the acorn ring attachment usual to papier mâché, bear a brass crown surmounted by a twisted ribbon whereon the name " Foster " is stamped in relief. Sometimes (as in the portrait of Pope Pius VI) he seems to have thought this sufficient signature; but on the other hand a pair in Mrs. Cairnes' collection, quite conventional for such an outlaw of the art as Foster, not only bear this Foster scroll but also the full signature of Foster at 125

Strand (for the best in all art ever drifts to London). Others, like one of George the Third, bear no clue either upon frame or card, except that the reddish-brown hue and general treatment of the gold lead even the least optimistic of collectors to write " Foster " on the back.

It is, however, fortunate that Foster for the most part signed freely in one way or another, for he had imitators even in his shade of brown. A pretty pair of silhouettes thus coloured and touched with gold in the collection of Captain Stanton, bears this interesting label :

" Bath,

Mr. J. S. Mitchell

Profilist

17 Union Street.

Executes Likenesses in a superior style of Elegance in Bronze Tints, &c., which contain the most forcible expression of Animation that can possibly be obtained by such mode of representing the Human Countenance."

Those not ashamed to glance on, like a female novel-reader, at a future chapter, will see that " a superior style of elegance " and " most forcible expression " are gems snatched from the Miers label. Mitchell, however, in altering the word " convey " to " contain " did not improve his copy ; nor can he be accounted better in his portraits than old Foster.

Foster was liberally old before he died in 1864, spanning the golden age of silhouette and the first birth of its supplanter in a single lifetime ; and I do not doubt that any keen soul who would risk a night in Derby could still hear at second-hand the centenarian's racy tales of " People I Have Painted."

If in considering those giants who made Silhouette an art in the late eighteenth century, Miers has been left till last, it is not by degree of merit, but rather on a principle exactly opposite.

Even were comparisons not duly odious, it would be hard to make a final judgment between Mrs. Beetham and her Leeds rival, Miers. Each had transcendent merits ; either was aiming at a rather different thing. Not mine, then, to award the palm. Taking my cue rather from that sphere where mere spatial position counts for most—I mean the Music Hall—I have, so to speak, given Mrs. Beetham the top, Miers the bottom, of the bill. Thus, like the artistes, each can claim to hold the premier position. . . .

John Miers, at any rate, was a fine craftsman,

quick to take a likeness and able to join obvious
fidelity with beauty of decorative effect. His work
falls rather naturally into three rough periods : Leeds,
early London, and nineteenth century. Of these the
first is easily best, not only in quality of rareness, but
in actual beauty. Head-dress, costume, laces—everything of course favoured the artist then, but quite
apart from this, Miers in Leeds and during those
first years in London before the dawn of a new
century (he seems to have moved about 1790) worked
in pure black, resisting the temptation of alluring gold.
Painted on oval slabs of chalk, the face dead black,
feathers or laces shading to transparent grey ; his
early portraits have a soft quality yet never sink, like
some by Charles, to mere prettiness or insipidity. In
the authentic frames of oval hammered brass they
make both in shape and delicacy an ideal decoration
on a plain cream wall. A glance at the specimen
here shown (plate x), a specimen backed with the rare
Leeds label, will prove in a moment the impossibility
of a comparison too often made. Miers, no less than
Mrs. Beetham, was capable of detail ; he was a
miniaturist of surpassing merit (plates xi and xxviii);
but whereas Mrs. Beetham's pride was clearly in the
wonderful minuteness of what one possibly may

Plate X.

PAINTED ON CHALK BY MIERS, LEEDS

Label unbroken : original brass frame.

X,

call her trimmings, Miers above all things was out for his effect. It must be said of him, indeed, that all his portraits, of whatever period, have an air of life that is utterly convincing.

The work of John Miers on first reaching London is scarcely to be distinguished from that of his earlier period. The label of course altered and the style of framing : but still the portrait was plain black. Miers unluckily dated but seldom ; only one specimen in my collection, the miniature on ivory, has a minute date, 1805, painted underneath the bust ; and it is thus difficult to say at what date he began the gilt work, which became almost a habit when he joined partnership with Field. So far, however, as my observation of specimens by Miers goes, it was not till the perruque had vanished that the gold appeared. Of unsigned silhouettes I possess two that show both gold-touching and perruques ; the first reputed to be Lord Howe, black and gold with a white stock, the other one of those rare but delightful soldiers with gay red coats and epaulettes of gold, which has in this case strayed on to the hair.

As to this last embellishment, condemned so heartily by that æsthete among silhouettists, Edouart, let it be said at once that Miers, with the later Hervé, was almost the only artist who could employ it without being vulgar. It cannot, indeed, be claimed that its addition improved either the truth or the decorative charm of his portraits, yet at its best it does gain an effect of intimacy which does not offend the casual critic and may have been delightful to relative or lover. The nicest specimen of this work that I have found is a curiously life-like portrait of a young man, painted upon chalk, with each fold of the coat and almost every hair of the head traced in a manner delicate almost beyond credibility (plate iii). The face itself, by now, is black no longer but of a dark brown, which makes me wonder whether Miers had not sat even for a moment at the feet of his new rival Foster.

What methods were or were not adopted by any profilist it is impossible or rash to say, for here was an art above all things of experiment ; but though Miers painted upon card, I have yet to learn that he ever cut a portrait out of paper. I have not even, with certainty, yet found a Miers painted upon glass. One, which was hopefully reported to me as " Napoleon " (a name that I have since erased, along with others upon sundry specimens, for reasons mainly of costume and period), has certainly the touch of Miers in his later manner. Indeed, if it be by another hand, the treatment of the scarf has almost gone beyond the limit of what one may call justifiable plagiarism. Certainly a striking and firm portrait, this silhouette is backed with wax of a pink-tinged yellow applied upon the glass : a further reason to regret the lack of label. Myself, I own to prejudice against this wax-backing, valued by some connoisseurs : it cracks on the least provocation and even when whole lends no charm that I can see to the original profile, nor was it much used by the best artists of the early period. Mrs. Beetham, it is true, a notable enough exception, employed a brownish-yellow wax as background now and then, for I have seen authentic pairs with the unbroken label, but to my mind this rather grimy shrine ruins the dainty portrait, which stands out so prettily against the white chalk of more normal specimens.

Miers, in any case, certainly painted upon ivory, and it is still possible to pick up delightful miniatures, under an inch long, dethroned no doubt from rings or lockets by unappreciative Victorians. These are usually signed " Miers " under the bust in writing of almost incredible minuteness. These vary from the pig-tail period, severely drawn in black with just the hair and ruffles melting to transparency, very

much like the Miers formula on chalk, on through
the early nineteenth century and London period of
that shown on pl. xxvii. and dated 1805, to specimens
with brown faces and elaborate gilt-touching. Mrs.
Fleming of Folkestone has in her collection a portrait,
in the middle period, of Sir Walter Scott, a miniature
gem apart from the interest of subject.

Some of these miniatures, by Mrs. Beetham and
the other giants of her art, have been spared in the
costly jewelled setting—lockets, boxes, rings—of
which their own age judged them worthy. Both
Mrs. Nevill Jackson and Mr. Francis Wellesley (pl. ix)
have specialized in this luxurious department, and one
may doubt whether the world holds many more of
these delightful trinkets among its stock of undis-
covered treasure-trove. Humble connoisseurs, or
those too late upon the scene, must thus console
themselves with the reflection, jaundiced and yet
philosophic, that frames are a mere accident (in
logic's sense) to the real silhouette-collector !

Other profilists there are ; workers on chalk, paper,
glass—of these last Jorden notably or Hamlet—who
cry for mention in a rapid survey of the great eighteenth-
century pioneers in this new and short-lived accomplishment, but I have mentioned all whose work is

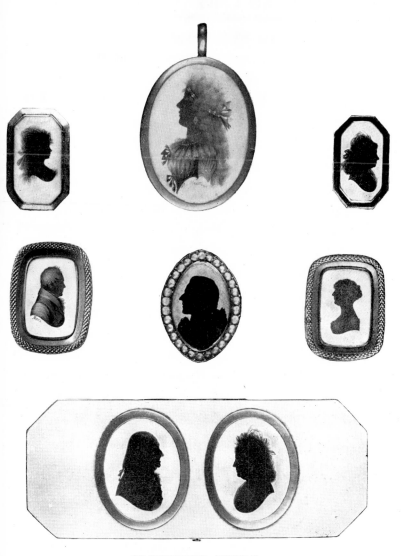

SILHOUETTE JEWELS

1 and 3 Ring, Miers ; 2 Locket, Mrs. Beetham ; 4 and 6, Brooch, Miers ; 5, Ring,
Gonord ; 7, Patchbox, Miers.
In the possession of Francis Wellesley, Esq.

likely to fall in the way of any average collector; most whose profiles were of the first rank in merit.

There are, however, perfect specimens to which, unhappily, no name can be attached with any certainty at all. Bereft of label and signature alike, the owner who can scribble great names at hazard on their back is either a vain idiot or Hope incarnate. Under this head (so far as I know) fall those splendid soldiers with their red coats and gold buttons, of which a beautiful example, from Mr. Wellesley's collection, appears upon pl. xxxii. It is of course the proper thing, *Page 170* indeed the only possible, to deprecate all bronze, and still more any colour, on a shadow-picture; yet when I look on these glorious officers in their mellow colours, nothing less scandalous than water-colour miniatures with blackened faces, I realize in shame how far even the most logical among us sacrifice our principles when faced by beauty.

IV

DECADENCE

CHAPTER IV

DECADENCE

SILHOUETTE, as I have shown, was always a thing of infinite variety. From its first birth, as a mere portrait cut from paper, there were variations; for quite apart from differences in size, half the earliest, indeed the most delightful specimens, were cut literally " from " white paper, leaving the face hollow, and laid on a black background so that the result was a black profile just as in the later process. Sad, indeed, that these masterly portraits are but seldom signed (though one in the Wellesley collection bears the name of Mrs. Harrington, and those of the 1790 period which have a dark grey backing may safely be ascribed to Torond, 18 Wells Street). Later artists, as time grew scarcer, doubtless found it easier to snick the portraits out in black, but it cannot be denied that the old white-cut process gave a greater softness. The lower lady on pl. iv, who is shrined in a unique old oval pewter frame, has a roundness and a fullness of face which,

achieved with such simplicity, has won the admiration of a dozen artists. More than one stubbornly
refuse to rank a Miers or a Mrs. Beetham above a
silhouette of such fine economy. Who shall decide ?
It is the old, old fight—luxurious charm *v.* classical
restraint, and I will not be referee.

In any case, these white hollow-cuts were possibly
thought freakish at first by advocates of Silhouette
as a mere shadow, often full-sized, cut from the black
paper : and in quite early days there had been other
variants. In Mr. Wellesley's collection there is a
convex glass that bears the head of George III in
black, and then behind it, in faint grey, his consort's,
very much as one might see them on a coin (pl. xii).
Another George III, presented to me by my friend
and fellow-collector, Mr. John Lane, is cut normally
in black, full-length ; but there is a clear mark at the
spot where his chest has once borne a spangled decoration. More curious than either is a specimen once in
the famous Montague Guest collection and now owned
by Mrs. Weguelin. This is inscribed in faint pencil,
barely legible : " Silhouette taken at Weimar in
1776–7 of Mdlle. Thun (? Thier) and of the society
that met at her house, amongst whom were Sir H.
Dalrymple, Sir Robert Keith, the Earl of Pembroke,

GEORGE III. & QUEEN CHARLOTTE

Painted on glass, probably by Charles (in the possession of Francis Wellesley, Esq.)

and General Harrison." The "society" was clearly taken each side of a table : nine heads in all, five upon one side and four on the other. Of these the front two, a man and a woman, are painted in black on a sheet of paper, whilst those behind are in a grey that intensifies to black only at the actual outline. These heads, that float bodiless in air like some dream-creatures, are cleverly drawn, but not too cleverly for any amateur of the days before Bridge ousted all the talents or turned them to professions. The nine members of this select society were, in fact, obviously painted by the tenth. Was this tenth person a ninth man (so to speak), or was it possibly just one lady to redeem Mdlle. Thun (? Thier) from the charge of a reckless social extravagance ?

Families, again, were sometimes taken at one time, though not in the grotesque way fashionable later. One of my earliest finds, when I first fared out from my Oxford rooms in the long quest for silhouettes, was a delicious quintette upon glass : father, mother, and three children, taken just after 1800 and probably by Rought of Oxford. They were a pleasant family but on such convex glass that daily I died deaths in fear of careless friends or housemaids, for what more terrible remorse for any man than to have broken a

73

treasure so intimate and gentle after survival of a century ? At last I sold it, thoroughly unnerved, and lately saw the Happy Family—a horrible regret to me—radiant as ever on its bulging glass in Mr. Wellesley's collection. . . .

All these variations there were in early specimens, but rare, and on the whole, Silhouette kept itself clean till somewhere round the twenties, as the most simple and yet not least effective of the arts. There were those who cut profiles, those who painted them on chalk, glass, ivory, or card, a few who toyed with coloured coats or chairs ; but always they retained the base idea that, work as they might upon the frills and laces, the face should be a shadow-portrait, plainly represented in black or some properly dark colour. This rule was observed even by that bold and not quite happy rebel, Phelps, who painted silhouettes with coloured dresses in chalk before 1790.

Who has ever been content ?—unless it were an animal. Philosophers, from the Greek tragedians down, point out that Man alone is never satisfied. The appetite appeased grows into a desire. Hunger paves the road to Gluttony, and through Comfort is the quick road from Need to Luxury. If Balaam's

donkey came to life again to-day, he would be happy
with a thistle or two and his own old coat : Balaam,
were he revived, would stand out for French cooking
and a telephone.   It is only a weak groping for excuse
which makes Man call the donkey stupid, so that on
the whole we may feel glad here to be just collectors,
not philosophers, and pass happily along.

Enough to say, then, that the nineteenth century
was far from satisfied. This art, that had arrived
with all the pomp of something hideously Greek,
seemed cheap to a new generation, and altogether far
too easy. The scissor-habit was so easily acquired :
snick, snick, quickness half the battle (everybody who
saw Granny practise is agreed on that), so why pay
anyone to do it ? Every one, in fact, was doing it.
The new toy had become a very ancient game.
Simplicity and cheapness were good reasons for
amateurs to try : the worst possible inducement for
anyone to visit a professional.

Thus the Professors, as they had now begun to be,
were doubtless driven to a new attraction, and what
more probable than gold ?

Miers it was, or Field, so far as I can tell, who first
began to add the gold as an accustomed thing.
Certainly these two, with Frith and Hervé, made the

best use of it. Miers especially, as I have said in the last chapter, by leaving the face plain brown and painting upon chalk, managed to lose hardly any dignity by what was certainly a far from wise departure ; and Field's work, during the time of partnership can scarcely de distinguished from that of his co-worker. Of those signed under the bust " Field, 2 Strand," some are in the brown and gold style ; others, less successful, have black faces touched with some pigment that is more a yellow than a gold, and certainly depressing. Cheerfulness, upon the other hand, was a strong point with Hervé farther down the street, at number 145. To his brown full-lengths he added gold of such a glow as to seem almost transparent, giving out light like Nijinsky's arms in " The Blue God." This shading he applied with rare discrimination, resisting the prevalent temptation towards overdoing it. By using it only upon one side of the body he gained a genuine effect of some one standing in a strong yellow light, and can probably claim first place among those who used gold-touching on the full-length portrait. Generally, but not always, a washed-in ground-work ended in a tree that topped the sitter's shoulder on the " lighted " side, and a solidly theatric gentleman who takes a pose

CUT SILHOUETTE, GOLD-TINTED
By Hervé (about 1830).

thus in one specimen stands in another before a curtain which more fittingly supplants the tree. Hervé often stamped his portraits, back or front, with his name and address, but I have not yet found a dated specimen. Young men, however, with hats like city chimney-pots and pulled-in waists to counteract a thrust-out chin (pl. xiii), reduce the date with something very much like certainty to 1830. Upon a slightly later head-and-shoulder portrait of a girl, in dark grey touched with black, the legend runs: "Hervé Artist, 172 Oxford Street and 248 Regent Street," so that I hope he had prospered. F. Frith, the last of this quartette which managed to use gilt without vulgarity, apparently is in the small band of provincials who meeting with Success have not been drawn by her to London. At any rate, I have not come across a specimen as yet that gives him a town gallery. One, very lavish in its gilt, is signed in full upon the ground-work, "F. Frith, Dover, Kent," and dated "1825." The 2, however, has been tampered with by some one who desired to own—or sell ?—a silhouette of Wellington, as which it was reported to me by a trustful dealer. Considered from the aspect of technique, it shows one very interesting feature. The white band that goes across

Page 76.

the soldier's chest is represented by a broad cut through his body from epaulette to thigh. The metal clasp (I speak as a fool) is thus painted on the actual card, though sword-hilt and scarf, cut from the paper, bridge this ruthless gash. It is certainly a quite original device and possibly justified by its success. More conventional and no less charming is the specimen which I have named " The Girl with the Bonnet " (pl. xiv). Frith in this case has merely cut an ordinary silhouette and then embellished it with gold-work of amazing fineness. A little softness has been gained for hair and lace by a few touches of brush-work upon the background, a trick probably unjustifiable by any strict canons drawn up for the art of Silhouette. Certainly, however, this little lady with her ringlets, her hat held shyly like a flower-basket, and those decorous trousers, stands triumphantly before her sundial to vindicate in innocence the shocking proposition that decadence can have its charm. She may not be pure silhouette, but she is an unqualified delight and we will throw no stones at her creator.

Of another profilist who cut portraits from the twenties onwards it is less easy to say pleasant things. Master Hubard, I fear, was of those luckless artists

THE GIRL WITH THE BONNET

Cut and gold-tinted by Frith, Dover.

who win a reputation during life, only to lose it shortly after death. The Londoners of his day loved him. At first an infant phenomenon, he soon grew up into a Gallery. The multitudinous examples extant prove it was the thing to have your profile taken at the Hubard Gallery. Above all, he took school-boys, squeezing their faces to shrew-like minuteness and topping them with an enormous cap. Those were the Spartan days, before a home revolved naturally around its youngest inmate, and one may imagine that a visit to the gallery was not unmixed delight. "What a pity," mothers would say, intent upon the current aim of Putting Boys into Their Proper Places, "that *you* are not clever like that gentlemanly and industrious little fellow."

Hubard was of his age and his age loved him dearly, both in London and New York. Thousands of little boyish heads, and hardly fewer full-length portraits, survive to prove his popularity. Mainly they are cut in plain black, but not a few of the ladies are elaborately gilt, and a few even venture on to white and blue One, of a K.G. unknown, shows the red uniform of an anæmic hue under a gold beard. Perhaps the kindest things to say of Hubard are that he was cheap and terribly unequal. He advertised " a strikingly correct

likeness with a frame and glass for one shilling . . . "
and as proof that he could hit off a good portrait one
need only look at the young dandy on pl. xv. This
is a firm piece of work, equal to Edouart except in its
flat treatment of the hair, and full of character. The
stick is painted, otherwise it is pure silhouette beyond
a doubt or cavil. Had the boy-wonder kept himself
straitly to this less flowery path, he might have been
accounted worthier of his distinguished, nay his
Royal, patrons.

Indeed, however, looking further afield, one may
admire in wonder his restraint or that of J. Gapp,
doggedly cutting plain black profiles at his tower on
the Chain Pier at Brighton. They were not gems of
art ; anatomically they admitted criticism ; but they
made a sincere attempt at holding up the old tradi-
tions. True, offered one and sixpence extra, he
would add the gold, but either he was not persuasive
or his patrons poor, for all that I have seen are plain.
In one a youth in a distinctly Edouart pose stands
by a vase upon an outdoor terrace (a favourite spot
with the great Frenchman, too), and I prefer the
portrait of " James Rosier, Junr., 1827 " (pl. xv).
Perhaps James, junior, was a vocalist, and certainly
his pose results in a sad heaviness towards the feet, yet

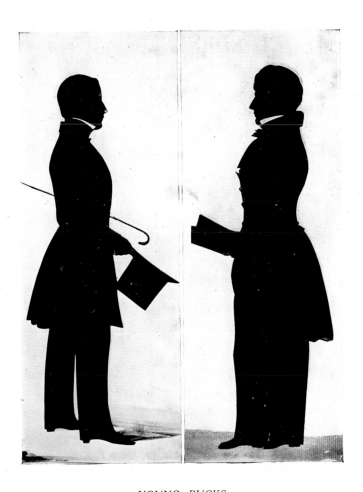

YOUNG BUCKS

Cut (1) by Master Hubard & (2) by Gapp (1827.)

xv.

there is firmness in the handling of his features and something original about the formula for showing buttons. This was a half-crown prudently laid out, and eighteenpence more might have spelt disaster.

Meanwhile, all around these devotees of the real Silhouette who kept the lamp alight through the dark thirties, professionals and amateurs were glorying in outrage more astounding at each new adventure.

It was a small enough thing to add gold eyebrows, gold lips, gold cheeks, to the already golden hair ; but that was only a beginning. Green, light or dark, for no reason to be gleaned from Nature's shadows, took the place of black or brown, whilst white was freely added to the gold. Foster, it has been seen, made bold experiments in colour, but usually with logic and good taste behind him. His imitators cared for none of these things, and so charming ladies of Victoria's era have come down to us with olive faces and gold ringlets : silhouette faces but gay-coloured gowns, black hands but gay-coloured faces ; or lapsing from the silhouette in nothing but their white silk stockings. One man of the sixties, duly cut from paper, stands before a background highly tropical in a grey suit and white shirt, sporting a gold seal, a red handkerchief, white hair (in parts), and a brick-coloured face.

Only stock, boots, and hat are black, so that one marvels why the portrait should be cut at all ; a silhouette by name but a bad miniature in fact.

And yet—and yet it does not do to dogmatize.

Time and again, upon the verge of framing a stern canon : " The real art of the silhouette is in the pure black shade, and every one who adds a colour to it is, as Edouart laid down, a vulgar mountebank," I have had an accusing vision. I have seen those brown Fosters so full of humanity, the fine gold-work of Miers, Spornberg's red defiant glow, and—above all, yes, let me now confess—two young Victorians in yellow maple frame, filling the room about them with the gentle fragrance of their restful age. They sit, these sisters, unconcerned by any wish to vote, to smash, to burn ; giving no thought to any problem but for those of their small social circle ; totally absorbed in the new song-album that has come down to them from London. Some one has told them once that they are strikingly alike, and this has pleased the elder. . . . Their dress is similar, with just enough variety for their admirers. Flowers are on the table, blue and yellow—can they be forget-me-nots ?—whilst pen and albums lend an air of culture. Sweet creatures of soft profiles and delicious corkscrews, for better or for worse their type has passed away : but here they are, by a profilist's art, better expressed for ever than in a score of tomes on the Victorian Age : (pl. xvi). *see over*

This picture (for it is no less, if by no other right than its fine composition) bears a legend : "The Misses Awdry, Lund House, Near Milksham : 1844." I hope they later took another name, for here are grandmothers of whom a man might properly feel pride.

Beaumont of Cheltenham, who painted them, perhaps went to Lund House upon the common basis of "Attendance Abroad Double." This, with his subject's charm, would then explain how he came to achieve a silhouette so far superior to his average bare-looking and stiff-cut production.

But—and here is my crux—save for the beads and topmost album, there is no spot of black about it ! They are a harmony in browns, these sisters, with just a touch of white for laces and two dim-red albums. Their faces are cut with a master's firmness, the eye-lashes touched in upon a dark cream background. Dignity and restfulness breathe in this whole portrait, which I would not change for fifty pure black Edouarts.

What then of our canon ? A compromise, I fear. Perhaps we may arrive at it by saying that *quâ* art (the don-like Latin tag gives me new courage) a silhouette should be no more than the pure shadow, anyhow as to the face, but that *quâ* charming decoration there is no possible objection to a prudently selected colour. No doubt Edouart was terribly artistic by all abstract canons when he produced that stiff and frugal tea-party which adorns pl. xli ; but I'm afraid it languishes in a portfolio, whilst I pay daily homage to my dear brown ladies. Madame Dorotti, too, in Ebury Street, owns among her private treasures a delicious study in dark green and white of a girl with all her dainty laces shown in touches so light that her hair peeps through their transparency. This is signed " W. M. Young del, 1836." Perhaps it is the work of an accomplished amateur, for Silhouette was taught in the young ladies' seminaries, nor in those days did every one who found a latent talent leap gaily at once into the professional arena. In any case, amateur or not, this lady of the olive hue will serve to emphasize our needed subdivision : pure Art —unadulterated Charm.

And colour, after all, was but the least heresy attached to their black art not less by countless

Page 222.

84

Plate xvi

THE MISSES AWDRY

Cut and painted by Beaumont, in browns.

itinerants than by innumerable amateurs. Paper or glass was not enough by now : silk, horn, wood, copper, glass were drawn into the use of Silhouette. Portraits duly cut in black were dressed elaborately with actual embroideries. Jewels and buttons were added recklessly in gold (sometimes, as with two owned by the Rev. Forster Brown, on glass). Novelty was even sought by cutting bodies off at that enormity of compromise, the three-quarter length. Coloured paper of every hue conceivable was tried. The early hollow-cut was revived and promptly robbed of all significance by gold-paint added to the black background. Tumblers were made with Nelson or Wellington imbedded, a silver silhouette, inside the thick white glass. The old-time profile was combined with hair-work, laid on a mirror, gummed to a slab of chalk : anything purposeless to gratify the wish for Something New. Skeleton leaves were obviously, then, another form of background, or iridescent paper recalling the crackers of our youth. Often an older formula was tried—and ruined. The beautiful old red-coat soldiers of the eighteenth century were thus sanction for young ladies all in colour save for a face apparently unwashed. In the same way that charming notion so prettily exploited by Charles or

Mrs. Beetham, the loved one's very shadow cast upon chalk placed behind, was turned into a horror by these later vandals. This was a full-length era—head-and-shoulders was probably accounted cheap !—and so gloomy-trousered men or shapeless-bodied boys were painted thinly on protruding glass, and the proud owner told to hang the whole " not exceeding five feet from a side light." The result possibly can be imagined : certainly it shall not be portrayed. Mrs. Bromley-Taylor owns the most pleasing example of this misguided industry that I have met. A marine background, with rocks and lighthouse, lends interest to the customary full-length figure. This picture is inscribed " by J. Woodham from Milverton : $A^o D^{ni}$ 1825," but I cannot help feeling that some one has blundered as to the equally usual directions, for in this case they run, " To be placed upon a south or back light not exceeding five feet in height. . . ."

More original, if no less superfluous, was another device invented, I think, in the later twenties by some unwitting anticipator of Bertillon. The sitter placed his or her thumb into some thick creamy substance and made thumb-prints upon the inside of a convex glass. These were duly scraped away, except so much as made the face or sometimes the cap, collar, dress, etc. ; and black was added to portray the rest, whilst one in the Wellesley collection has gold and mauve touches upon a blue thumb-printed base. The result seems to me more quaint than beautiful, but these silhouettes, entitled "Thumb-print," are greatly accounted by a few collectors.

The next step was just as inevitable then as it now seems incredible. Silhouette, robbed of its old simple dignity, an art no longer, must become a trick. There had always been machines for taking profiles. Allusion has been made to these already, and on a stray page (from what old magazine, I wonder, of the twenties?) I have lately found this rather illuminating passage : " Next to this is a plain black profile, to which I can say, ' *That's me.*' I took it into my head the other day to walk into a shop and suffer the *machine*, as they call it, to be passed over my visage ; and here I am quite *black in the face*, with a smart ebonized frame, and an inner gilt edge, *all for four shillings !* What a depreciation of the fine arts, if indeed this can be said to belong to them ! " But in this passage, which throws an interesting light upon the price of those now precious ebonized black frames, the reference is to something in the nature of a long and flexible rod so contrived that one end of it transferred to paper the contour over which the other end was passed (Edouart speaks scornfully of the tickling caused by "a piece of wire"); and much the same, no doubt, was meant by J. P. Tussaud, who, a showman by hereditary right, drew London of the twenties to his wax-works with the vague announcement : " . . . has a machine by which he takes profile likenesses." Hervé equally boasts on a label to have " taken the likenesses of upwards of 12,000 persons " by the use of Hankin's " patent machine."

Quite a different contrivance, however, was upon the market before Victoria was Queen. Perhaps no clearer hint as to its nature can be given than by the following announcement, culled from the back of an apparently late Georgian profile :

" Now Exhibiting,
In Apartments over the shop of
Mr. LIDDELL, Shoe Maker,
Corner of the Market Place, Huddersfield.

PROSOPOGRAPHUS,
The Automaton-Artist.

This splendid little figure possesses the extra-ordinary power of drawing by Mechanical

means the likeness of any Person that is placed
before it in the short space of one Minute.
It is hoped that the Inhabitants of Huddersfield will come forward with their usual spirit,
to encourage a piece of ingenuity at once so
novel and curious.

A likeness in Black for one shilling,
Coloured from 7s. 6d. upwards.
Open from Ten till Eight."

Here if ever, surely, is a use for the old tag: "Comment is superfluous." Indeed, the time is better spent
in sadly throwing back the fancy to forty years before,
when all the modish bucks and belles were swarming
to the galleries of Charles, Rosenberg, or Mrs. Beetham.
Art is long—but popular caprice is short. Enough to
say, for those who have no Greek, that this Prosopographus, with the quite subtle tinge of magic in its
sound, is nothing but a mongrel word to mean face-
delineator: nor can I resist a vicious wonder what
intervals exactly the "splendid little figure" needed
for its meals. . . .

Whether it is this particular automaton to which
Sam Weller alluded in his historic love-letter—" in
much quicker time and brighter colours than ever a
likeness was took by the profeel macheen . . . altho'

it *does* finish a portrait and put the frame and glass on complete, with a hook at the end to hang it up by, and all in two minutes and a quarter "—is a question that may be left to Mr. Matz and the Dickensians.

By the side of this and kindred pieces of ingenuity (which I am utterly confident Huddersfield encouraged with its Usual Spirit), there is almost nothing to be said against the following :

"PERFECT LIKENESSES.

No. 4, Wells Street, Third door from Oxford Street. (By His Majesty's Special Appointment.)

Jones' Reflecting Mirrors, at One Guinea each, for taking Likenesses in Profile or full Face : also, Landscapes and Views from Sea, &c.

They are made on so easy a Plan, that a child of ten years of age cannot fail to take a perfect likeness with them . . .

Perfect Likenesses taken in Miniature Profile at 2*s.* 6*d.*, and painted on Glass or Chrystals, in a stile of superior elegance, from 5*s.* to 18*s.* each.

Miniatures neatly painted from Three to Five and Ten Guineas each.

N.B.—Such who wish to see the effect of the above instrument pay One shilling each, which will be returned on purchasing of either the above instrument, or sitting for an Impression Plate Likeness."

A VICTORIAN YOUNG LADY

Cut silhouette touched with white paint.

This advertisement, found in a scrap-book, is unluckily not dated, but its type and general appearance point to somewhere around 1825.

By the thirties, in any case, Silhouette was nothing but a freak. Endless itinerants of little merit divided up the less sophisticated parts of the Homeland between them. F. W. Seville cleverly staked out a claim on Shrewsbury and the Midland schools, where he adorned prim-looking scholars with unconvincing gold. Others visited America. London probably had proved a little cold : all ready now, the fickle jade, for a more hideous darling, the daguerreotype. Silhouettes grew cheaper—and more thick with gold. Sometimes, if left plain black, the lines and shadows were pushed out from behind, to form a high relief. Fuzzy-looking ladies pranced about on horses that nowadays would be condemned by the authorities. Line, form, massed effect : silly thoughts like that had vanished ! Everything was niggly, tortured. The highest praise remained for something *new*.

At the British Museum, in the Mediæval Room (for humour has no place in a museum), there may be found a piece of stone which bears a natural white profile on it. Black plaster has been added above to round off the skull and on it is inscribed : " O, my country ! "

No doubt it is meant to be Mr. Pitt, but it would have been Chamberlain if he had only been invented. This freak-portrait, which is described as *Lusus Naturæ*, seems to me the last comment upon Silhouette. The time had come now for aquarium or pier. Never had any art so swift a decadence.

Yet—did it fall maybe with its epoch? Did it, like painting, find costume and atmosphere alike too ugly? Did it only hide its dainty head until a fifth George brought back "Elegance and Taste"?

These questions are too deep for me, and I am prejudiced. I fling the horrors of my dear art into deep portfolios and hang its best work only on my walls. If I am asked for the Victorians, I point blatantly to the Exceptions: Beaumont's two sisters, the Foster soldier, Frith's girl with the bonnet, or another child who stands in an incredible costume with a sick-looking bird upon her index-finger. White ribbons, white stockings, and beautiful white drawers relieve a dress sombre otherwise beyond the wearer's years. She stands between two mountains and around her there hop other, less favourite, birds. Or maybe they are tufts of grass. . . .

Well, well: she is very charming, and sometimes I wonder what Miers would have made of anyone with such a bonnet (pl. xvii). One thing is certain, neither he nor any of the great profilists of 1790 would ever have attempted more than a mere head-and-shoulder. This full-length mania was no small portion of the Decadence. But what restraint or classicism could anyone expect in an age that worshipped Berlin wool-work and made a religion of antimacassars ? Let us be thankful, rather, that there *are* exceptions.

V
EDOUART

CHAPTER V

EDOUART

THINGS were not by any means so desperate as this with Silhouette, although the gold-work reigned supreme, when Augustin Amant Constance Fidèle Edouart came, with almost managerial solemnity, upon the scene. Before his discovery in 1825 that he could take a profile, he had worked portraits in hair. He was assuredly therefore an artist, and he meant no one to forget it. He cut himself proudly adrift from all former practitioners of silhouette (a word imported by himself, though borrowed from Lavater), and set himself with confidence to the task of placing his art in its due position. It is only one among poor Edouart's countless tragedies that most of Silhouette's enormities were perpetrated *after* his renaissance. . . .

Edouart needs understanding. It is lucky therefore that he wrote a book. Had he written five we should have learnt no more about the man, for he who cried, " O that mine enemy would write a book," knew that before a second venture the art of self-concealment dawns. Edouart wrote only one, and it is a full revelation. The fellow struts, magnificent, complacent, through its hundred and sixteen small pages. Grievances, yes : he was not treated with a due respect by many : but what of that ? It was their ignorance ! He got his due from Royalty ! Edouart gave us the term silhouette, and never thought of the word swank. . . .

He had got, in any case, the secret of being accepted very much at his own valuation. An ex-soldier of Napoleon, a refugee in a strange country, he yet claims that, when this great gift of Silhouette had been revealed to him, his first customer was no less than a Bishop. This was Dr. Magendie of Bangor. The sting, however, of this tale is in the fact that forty copies of the silhouette were ordered at five shillings, and all the family was done as well, so that it is possible that Edouart, no less than human in his self-deceptions, forgot the earlier patrons of humbler origin or smaller orders.

The book wherein Edouart unveils ingenuously his tragedies and triumphs is entitled " A Treatise on Silhouette Likenesses." Published in 1835 by Long-mans, it is now extremely scarce, partly no doubt

Plate XVIII.

MR. REILLY (?), MAGDALEN COLLEGE, 1827.

Cut by Edouart.

xviii.

by reason of a small edition but also because it has been broken up by dealers or scrap-book compilers tempted with its many lithographs in silhouette by a Cork printer. Edouart, being of those who regard their title-page as a cheap advertising medium, describes himself as " Silhouettist to the French Royal Family and Patronized by His Royal Highness The Late Duke of Gloucester and the principal Nobility of England, Scotland, and Ireland. . . ."

Edouart's troubles concerned themselves partly with customers who were either dissatisfied with their own faces or refused to pay. For one of these last, indeed, he retails with obvious pleasure how he devised a fitting punishment. Taking the unmistakable likeness of this mean patron, he made it end, from the waist downwards, as a corkscrew. Adding a ring (all cut, of course) by which the top-hat hung on to a hook, he called the whole :

PATENT SCREW FOR FIVE SHILLINGS

and hung it in his window, for every one to see. This story he tells in a chapter gloomily entitled " Grievances and Miseries of Artists."

A much greater tribulation, however, than this was

the treatment received by the sensitive profilist from those with whom he came socially in contact. Feeling deeply that his craft had been a despised one, he was at pains to show how different all other silhouettists were. These, by a charming Gallicism, he accuses of " Gothic taste," whilst he constantly refers to himself as an Artist and seldom grudges a big A. Nobody must think that he took up his art after a long search for some way to make money. No ! Dining with some friends, he criticized a much admired machine-cut silhouette. " Could he do better ? " the daughters of the house teasingly inquired. Spurred by their taunts to "a fit of moderate passion," he could, and did. He snipped a profile— with " facility and exactness "—from an old envelope, and blacked it from a candle-snuffer. In such a drawing-room way did Edouart fittingly embark upon his art, taking the hideous risk of being " cut from society " ; and he narrates how his " talent showed itself so strongly " that not only did he over-work, but even in his dreams " was cutting likenesses of great personages, Kings, Queens, etc."

Ah ! in those words lie Edouart's real tragedy. His poor swollen head never quite recovered from royal patronage. It was in 1830 that he took the

likenesses of Charles X and all his suite at Holyrood.
Even an ex-king was too much for Edouart, and
from that day nobody in England was quite polite
enough. Imagine that he, Silhouettist to the French
Royal Family, should be "placed on a level with the
caravan man" or subjected to the insults of ordinary
people who, attracted by the new word silhouette,
came into his studio and flounced out saying, "Oh,
they are all black shades!" Conceive a mere land-
lady refusing to receive "a man who does these
common black shades"! Picture to yourself the
feelings of an artist, walking arm-in-arm with "friends
who moved in circles of high life" and hearing the
riff-raff remark, "Who can she be, that lady with
the black shade man?" . . . Edouart, a soldier
and a gentleman, could not inflict such insults upon
his acquaintance and began to walk alone, with the
result that "persons of high rank in society" often
accused him of an unseemly pride.

But much worse was to come.

Received at length in one town with all the pomp
which he thought nothing but his due, Edouart was
lent a house by the very governor of the castle, who
hoped that the boards "might be strong enough
for the exercise of his profession" and the crowds it

would attract, urging him to practise only on the ground floor in mere prudence. Here was flattery indeed! Edouart, one may see, was in the seventh heaven, thinking it a dream. Then—read this with care, ye who think Juliet's silly accident to be real tragedy!—then the governor stripped off his coat and suggested a preliminary practice. On relentlessly the drama moves, until the governor, amazed, reads out the letter of introduction which had made him receive the profilist with such respect: " I recommend to your notice Monsieur Edouart, the famous *Pugilist.* . . ."

Enough! Those with imagination can supply the rest.

It may be said, however, that England, although obviously rated as an inartistic country well content with the profile-machine and very different from the French Royal Family, yet supported Edouart in gallant manner. No author, no actor, no divine, no soldier, too famous for his studio, whilst at Oxford and Cambridge, which he particularly favoured, the most learned dons did not disdain to have their profiles taken. One little bundle of Oxford Edouarts that has come down as a whole includes such names as Dr. Buckland the geologist, holding a prehistoric-

MR. LISTON IN HIS OWN CHARACTER

Cut by Edouart.

seeming skull in hand ; Blanco White the theologian, seated in a chair ; the Rev. John Gutch, historian ; and Benjamin Parsons Symons, Vice-Chancellor of the University, all taken in the one year 1828. Nor was America less kind, for here too, when he transferred his studio thither in 1839, the greatest of the land surged to his studio. Mrs. Nevill Jackson has lately had the pleasure of returning to the White House as a gift the silhouette of John Tyler, President of the United States, taken there by Edouart in 1841.

It might be thought, then, that Edouart would have been a contented man and not have girded so bitterly at the poor public or needed so terribly to be " upon his dignity." Perhaps he found a greater tolerance in the years after his book's publication. If not, one can only think there is a great truth hidden under that old nursery formula of Something to Cry for Presently. This man who so persistently had snivelled about details suddenly was struck down by a serious blow.

Returning homeward in 1849, after ten triumphant years, bearing with him his precious folios, a duplicate of every portrait he had ever taken, he suffered shipwreck off the coast of Guernsey, an old man in his sixties, and lost all but a few of the countless specimens that were to be his monument for ever. Broken-hearted, he seems never to have practised any more. The rescued folios, fourteen in all, he gave to Frederica Lukis of Guernsey, who had been kind to him. He died, this tragic comedian, in 1861. Dickens would have loved him, and I sometimes think there is in his life a novel ready for some lesser hand.

Edouart is the most easy of all profilists to " spot," because he was consistent to one method. He cut portraits in black paper. Apart from this, he usually signed and he was generous with labels. Sometimes, though not as a rule on his best specimens, he stamped the name and date with a die-stamp—not very dignified for one who spelt art with a capital. On one in my possession he has written, after " Augn. Edouart fecit. 1829," the full instruction : " No. 111 Oxford Street, Entrance in Regent Circus." This, however, the portrait of an elderly gentleman standing, some way after Napoleon, on the sea-shore, is one glorified with a hand-painted background, and the artist probably would not here grudge a little extra trouble. Of these painted backgrounds, and their less expensive variant the lithographed, it is not easy to say much in praise artistically, though of course to the collector they are nice specimens, as rarer. This sea-shore specimen is probably the most successful, because it naturally involves a very low horizon. Indoor scenes are frankly horrible, and their looped curtains or sham-classic columns utterly ruin the silhouette's effect. It is odd that Edouart, so stern about gilt on the plain black shade, should have encouraged this astounding habit. In the course of his remarks upon the bronzing of costume or hair, which he nicely terms a harlequinade, " gold hair, coral ear-rings, blue necklaces, white frills, green dress," there occurs this passage : " It must be observed that the representation of a shade can only be executed by a shadow . . . consequently all other inward additions produce a contrary effect. . . . Every artist or real connoisseur will allow with me that when Nature is to be imitated, the least deviation from it destroys what is intended to be represented." Edouart undoubtedly was right as to the bronzing, but it has always seemed to me that these remarks might equally be used of his own painted backgrounds. A silhouette is *ex hypothesi* the shadow of a man seen with a strong light behind him. Edouart usually, though by no means always, arranged the background so that the figure stood against the skyline or an open window, but by his own canon as to Nature, one may fairly ask why in a room like that upon pl. xx humans and dogs should seem a dead-black shadow whilst walls and furniture remain light brown. The best effect is certainly obtained when he gummed the profile on a plain cream card, omitting the elaborate backgrounds which he describes as by " Artists, and I may say not inferior ones. . . ."

Page 108

Edouart, moreover, cut full length. Certainly his labels offer " Profile Bust : 1*s.*," but the figure was perhaps considered his own speciality, for I have only found two busts in my long silhouette-hunt and only fifty occur among the new-recovered folios. Indeed, on this point he is no less firm than about the bronzing. " The figure adds materially to the effect and combines with the outline of the face to render, as it were, a double likeness." No doubt the artist had an air, and I imagine that the scarcity of head and shoulder portraits may be largely due to the contempt with which he would receive an order for the shilling bust. " Of course, madam, if you do not wish to pay five shillings, but in my opinion the figure adds . . ." and so forth, by the book !

It may be questioned whether he was wise, for

frankly anatomy is not quite his strongest point. Or would it be fairer to say that the shadow treatment will not brook foreshortening ? I own a truly hideous signed Edouart of 1837, a seated man of most chaotic shape, and even Mr. Connor, himself a portrait-painter, admitted to me that the hind leg of his beloved " Musician " is what the vet. would label gummy. It is possible that Edouart's chief attraction to the full-length profile was in the fact that it had been largely ignored by his great predecessors. Certainly Rosenberg advertises full-length family pieces, but I never met a specimen. Torond alone, of the earlier profilists, seems to have loved the full-length : and it is educational to compare his musician (pl. xxix) with Edouart's (Frontispiece). Perhaps Page 148 " Art and Accuracy " may sum up the contrast. Torond, indeed, was a master of decorative effect and each of his compositions is a separate delight.

Where Edouart was quite supreme is in his sense of character. This would account for his success in studies of child-life (pl. xxiii). He had the first gift Page 118. of a portraitist : he could portray and explain in a single illuminating moment. We know an Edouart subject as we know a Sargent : the soul is there no less than the mere shell. Edouart had a fine control of the scissors, but he had more than that, he had an eye for the important feature. None of his portraits, it may be, fall definitely beneath the head caricature, yet in many of them he good-humouredly betrays the human weakness under an expression. In his treatise there is a silhouette, "Checkmate," which but for its printed background might be ranked ideal. A genial old worthy, clinging still to the old-fashioned perruque and resting his gouty leg on a convenient footstool, leans back contentedly, a smile upon his lips, and helps himself to snuff. Opposite this self-complacent victor sits a younger man with very worried look, who hangs a listless, indecisive hand above the chess-board that nowhere shows a sign of hope. This is a fine thing. Equally good is the musician, happily absorbed in his own improvising (pl. i) or the young undergraduate (pl. xviii) superb in the calm confidence with which he holds his new cap out to a world full of possibilities and rests easily upon his beautifully shod feet. And almost better is the portrait of " Mr. Liston in his Own Character " (pl. xix), no doubt to distinguish it from one of the actor in his famous part Paul Pry: " I hope I don't intrude." Perhaps an expert might just cavil at the backmost leg, but the spectator's eye is caught

"PLATE XX"

XX.

A FAMILY

By Edouart, 1831.

first by the masterly roundness of feature, the easy pose, the firm tackling of the hands, the whole portrait's wonderful convincing, life-like quality.

Edouart was certainly unequal, but at his finest he is incomparably the best of those who literally cut profiles from paper in the nineteenth century. With the delicate artistry of Mrs. Beetham on glass or of Miers upon plaster he has no connection, and therefore one need not compare him with those great predecessors whom in his self-laudation he doggedly ignored. Enough to say that he soared far above his own contemporaries or any cutters who have yet come after.

Besides portraits of chance callers, Edouart achieved some fancy cuttings—the temptation of St. Anthony, the murderer, street scenes, &c.—and also advertised profiles of famous characters. This item on his labels naturally explains the many duplicates that still exist of anyone so popular as Dr. Simeon of Cambridge, who was depicted in no less than ten attitudes, many of them in the pulpit with hand dramatically raised to emphasize a point.

Edouart also did groups and was particularly proud of them. Here again he studiously ruled out all except the bad among his predecessors, and in his treatise gives a burlesque cutting of a " Family in a Row," intended to sum up the group-work of profilists before he himself arrived with his big A. This cutting, dwindling in size from papa to the dog (called Bijou), is certainly amusing but means less than nothing. No doubt such horrors were perpetrated daily in Edouart's own time, but profilists of forty years before had taken groups that make his stiff collections look like something by a feeble amateur. That glorious Burney family of Mr. Wellesley's, the family of Mrs. Wyatt's, how graceful these and a score more appear beside those stilted "natural" groups of which poor Edouart was so intensely proud ! They sit beneath their curtains, unashamed, at table, nor do they pretend to be all in anything but the same plane. Edouart's people, a full dozen often, make the absurd claim that they are alive. They all indulge at once in ill-assorted pastimes. One sews, another plays diabolo, a third holds flowers ; the children romp with whip or hobby-horse ; and baby sleeps uncomfortably upon a pillow. Large ancestral portraits sometimes hang in silhouette on the brown-painted walls. It is all worrying, illogical, and ugly.

No need here to go into the ground upon which

110

EDOUART

Edouart based his claim to have revolutionized the group in Silhouette. The easiest, if also the unkindest, refutation of the fact itself will be to reproduce a group of the best period and also—for let us be fair even when we are unkind—one of the best Edouart groups that I have so far found. The specimen reproduced upon pl. xx is certainly far better than Page 108. that which Edouart himself chooses to illustrate his high claims in the Treatise. That shows a wife and husband with six children, each of the last in a state of action near delirium. The two eldest play La Gráce, the next forges across the room with his toy horse; then one who stands upon a chair and holds a morsel for the dog to snatch; the three-year-old is swinging her doll hectically; lastly baby climbs its mother like a Matterhorn and snatches at her nose; all this before a bleak window looped with a balloon-like curtain. Compared with this, my specimen has almost dignity. This is a superior home, and Edouart (one guesses) felt in his own element. One may imagine his small talk of even more distinguished sitters as he ordained, with all an artist's firmness, that the youngest daughter should hold a flower up towards her stern elder, equally cold to the dog's adoration. Why, this is 1831, only

111

one year after that great visit to the French Royal Family! The very signature seems bolder. . . . In this amazingly large group, which measures two and a half feet across, the brown stool and table are cut out and gummed on to the card. Perhaps they ranked as "extra cutting," but, going back to Edouart's canon of Nature, it is possible to wonder why one piece of furniture should be in black shadow and another not. The fact is that this whole idea of the brown painted room was an abomination. With the figures themselves, as usual, Edouart has been successful. The swagger of the boy-rider is delightful, and one can hear the uncle, who believes in keeping a lad in his place, retort: "Ah! but you should have seen *me*. . . ." The mother's hair and nose, I much regret to chronicle, have been touched up with paint, each in a manner to improve her looks, and here we must blame, not the stern scissor-loving Edouart, but that vanity inherent in his subjects which he so frequently laments.

Yet when all that can be has been said in praise of each single figure, turn to the group upon pl. xxv, cut by an amateur about five years before Edouart's so-called renaissance, or to the beautifully formal tea-party upon pl. xxi. This perfect specimen by

"Plate xxi"

GROUP PAINTED BY TOROND

(In the possession of Mrs. Alec Tweedie.)

Torond belongs to Mrs. Alec Tweedie, and others like it are in the collections of Mr. Wellesley and Mrs. Wyatt. This table formula, in fact, was one adopted by Mrs. Patience Wright and all the great profilists of the eighteenth century, Torond, Gonord, and that skilful amateur of the art, Goethe. Few, I think, who duly look on this picture and that can doubt that Edouart, however much he may have improved upon the Family-in-a-Row formula that he sets up as convenient skittles, fell very far indeed behind his great predecessors in handling of the group.

Silhouette, in fact, is by its nature an art of convention, and just as this great cutter could not see that it would never express foreshortening in single figures, so did he fail to realize that it was not adapted to expressing various figures upon different planes. His efforts to show distant people by smaller size and a great sea of intervening carpet are seldom convincing and never artistic.

Short of the seated-at-a-table formula, which surely is pleasant enough in its formality, it seems to me that if families must be taken together (and it appears they must) some other of the older methods is better adopted. I have already spoken of five little heads on a protruding glass. The same idea was some-

times used on paper, and a specimen by Adolphe of
Brighton may be found on pl. xxiv. This is painted
in a blue-green tint that he affected, good work in
itself but of an even greater interest as document
in favour of heredity. Poor dear things; the
girls especially, all doomed to papa's nose. I
often wonder how they all fared in the fight
with life. Mrs. Wyatt, who has a small collection of profiles in her treasure-house of early
glass near Worthing, owns a delightful and earlier
family (ancestral I believe), each member set in a
separate oval of the large brass-studded, papier
mâché old frame, like that which holds the family,
probably by Field, on pl. xxviii. Another method,
quainter if less beautiful, is seen in Mr. Wellesley's
collection : parents and half a dozen children painted
inside eight tiny glass bosses, waxed at the back and
looking almost like round bullets in their wooden
frame.

Personally, at the risk of shocking those who set
no limit to clan sentiment, I incline to think that more
than two people never should be taken in one
silhouette. The early groups at table are charming
by very reason of their stiffness, and possibly exception might be made in favour of a fancy subject.

A HAND-SCREEN (xviii Century.)

Among my dearest treasures are, in fact, two eighteenth-century screens painted with delicious caricatures of beaux, belles, and beldams at a dance and musicale respectively. Here I would have not one figure less, and though a great deal has been lost in reproduction, I cannot resist one of them, pl. xxii, as proof of how delightfully a mass of figures may be used without, like Edouart, attempting the impossible : Reality. Equally, of later date, I saw once in a shop the most colossal silhouette, all gilt and brown, of probably the forties. A race-course scene, with horses, jockeys, stewards, nota-bilities, a perfect gem of its preposterous own kind, and on its way to Germany. Poor England, all that is worst in her was made in Germany, and all that was best is swiftly making there ! Paris, Germany, and the United States are quickly draining England of its Georgian treasure, and soon—I do not doubt— the day of the Victorians will come.

But I digress. . . .

Perhaps, before this lengthy chapter ends, some mention should be made of the duets that strengthen me in my heresy expressed. First, then, such eighteenth-century delights as that which appears in Lavater, or one of the same period belonging

Page 114 .

115

to Major-General D'Oyly Snow : Sir Thomas D'Oyly
seated at a table lecturing his son who stands,
a candle set between them, underneath a formal
curtain. Then that of Beaumont on pl. xvi, to
which I have paid a full tribute in the proper place,
or a quaint group by Driscoll, before a painted
Dublin background, of a patrician who gives alms to
an old Jewish beggar with a dejected hound. And
lastly let the catalogue end with Edouart's tea-party,
dated 1826, and taken at 4 Colonnade, Cheltenham.
It may be said of Edouarts, in a catch-phrase, the
earlier the better ; yet though this is among his
earliest, I am afraid its composition will not bear
comparison with the Sisters by Beaumont, one of those
profilists whose coloured work he so bitterly labelled
with the fine word " bigarrade."

Poor Edouart ! A man so terribly aware of slights,
despite the *habit de toile cirée* of which he boasts, should
have adopted almost any other trade, or even stuck
to his hair portraits.

His was in many ways a tragic life, although its
sadness was as frequently home-made, but the last
act in his one authentic tragedy, the loss of his
precious folios, unrolled itself, oddly enough, but
lately. Mention has been made of a Lukis family in

Guernsey that gave hospitality to the poor ship-wrecked profilist, as of a Frederica Lukis to whom he gratefully presented such duplicates as had been rescued from the sea. Nobody more remote than a son of this Frederica suddenly appeared upon the scene from Guernsey, like some magician gifted with a time-machine, bearing with him—or offering to bring—the fourteen long-lost folios ! This treasure Mrs. Nevill Jackson was lucky enough to secure. Over five thousand British portraits, taken chiefly in Bath, Cheltenham, and Scotland, with scarcely fewer taken in America, are here found dated, named, and sometimes with an odd detail as to the sitter's height or weight. In each case also there is a note as to the place in which the portrait had been taken. Through the kindness of Mrs. Nevill Jackson I am able to reproduce a sample page (pl. xxiii). These *Page. 118.* are the " Daughters of General Sir Ralph Darling, 8th Sept., 1836," and are named—from left to right— " Miss Agnes Darling, 3 years : 3 ft. 2 in. Miss Caroline Darling, 7 years : 4 ft. Miss Amelia Darling, 4¾ years : 3 ft. 6 in." It was Edouart's boast, by the way, that all his portraits after 1827 were true to military scale.

So early as 1835 he speaks of his gallery as

comprising above 50,000 likenesses ! Most profilists, it will be gathered from the chapter upon " Labels," professed to keep the original shades—will time finally yield the treasure of Miers' duplicates ?—but Edouart clearly possessed a genius for system. The name of each sitter was entered in five different places ! Not to be outdone, Mrs. Nevill Jackson has compiled an alphabetic list of the five thousand names found in these British folios, and slowly no doubt the portraits will filter back into the homes of their originals' descendants. This, one likes to think, will be as balm to the soul of too sensitive Edouart, which must have suffered agonies in those late Victorian days when silhouettes were being torn, burnt, thrown away on all sides and their frames used for Christmas Number presentation plates. So after all we may ring down the curtain on a happy ending.

A PAGE FROM EDOUART'S RECOVERED FOLIOS.

(In the possession of Mrs. Nevill Jackson).

VI

CUPID AND
SILHOUETTE

CHAPTER VI

CUPID AND SILHOUETTE

SILHOUETTE should certainly have been called the Art of Love, had not Ovid long since turned that pleasant title to a baser use.

For, after all, what product of man's handicraft should Cupid smile upon more naturally ? Hung in auspicious pairs, they breathe romance, these little shadows, and the sound of long-past but undying kisses rises from them in the night. Businesslike collectors weed out ruthlessly : " a pair of Fosters—yes, the man bad but the girl worth keeping " : shattering for ever who shall say what ancient vows or separating may-be young hearts which a cruel world had joined but once—upon a secret visit to the profilist's. These are no chance pairs that come down to us nor are they always man and wife. They are as often Cupid's gage ; and who are we to separate the two ? The lover of his treasures can almost hear departing visitors remark : " What lovely things ! yes, but one or two terribly unworthy ! " And yet—yet he

121

remembers where he bought it, with what joy he brought it proudly home, what happy days cling to its ancient frame ; yet he remembers it has hung for who shall say how long fronting that other shadow upon which the profilist bestowed such better art. . . . No ! if I see connoisseurs whose specimens are all first class, I give whole-heartedly my admiration, but I keep back my trust. They are not men, and I dislike machines.

On, on, before I horrify with yet more painful tales of soldiers and young damsels, swept on to tacks opposite by a collector's whim, joined by no passion of their earthly lives, yet linked so long in shadow-land that the collector must not break asunder. . . . These be the harrowing rewards of such as truly love the shadows of dear people turned to dust ; most intimate, most sentimental, of all symbols brought down by the flood of time. Pass by with a sigh of pity, reflecting each on his own beautiful delusions.

Cupid was present, so the old prints show, when the first Grecian invented silhouette by tracing on a wall the shadow of his dear one : and Cupid has been present ever since. Adolphe, indeed, who came from France to Brighton with his art, printed a long rambling poem on his labels, entitled " The Origin

A FAMILY

Painted on one card by Adolphe, of Brighton.

of Profiles." Apart from a passionate lyricism, its chief point is an odd lack of full stops, so that for my purpose it will be enough to quote the opening words :

" *'Twas Love, 'twas all-inspiring Love. . . .*"

This was a fact that those who cut fancy subjects never had far from their minds. One of my earliest specimens shows a large, white heart filled with formal decoration ; and underneath a white-cut lion which submits with natural boredom to be garlanded by Cupids I find the following quotation :

> " *Love vaunts his universal Sway.*
> *Earth, Sea, and Air his Pow'r obey.*
> *Lord of the Lion Heart he reigns*
> *And leads him bound in rosy Chains,*
> *Meek as the Slave, with humblest Duty*
> *To crouch before the Feet of Beauty.*"

This is, no doubt, an amateur attempt, and here Cupid is more at home than with the busy profilists intent on their five shillings. To the methodical collector amateurs are no more than a bugbear ; they seldom sign, and if they do it is confusing ; but after all, professionals are only amateurs accepting money and much of the best in all art has been

Page 36

achieved for love. Mrs. Leigh Hunt cut some delightful portraits in white paper; Lane Kelfe of Bath, who painted a few charming silhouettes (pl. v), was probably not a professional; and I have lately been allowed by the kindness of a descendant to see a dozen profiles by John Phillp, who took them in Soho before 1793, where he died at the early age of twenty-six. It may be said of these that they would disgrace no professional and, being unsigned, vastly puzzle any connoisseur. Painted for the most part on a reddened card, the faces are of a dead black, the hair sometimes touched in silver-seeming pencil with all of Mrs. Beetham's fineness, and the whole portrait has a fine virility of touch. All these have under the bust an inked line parallel with the black mass; a formula of recognition. This is work in the first rank, and would have been no whit improved if he had taken money. . . .

Princess Elizabeth, George III's daughter, was another amateur of real distinction, with this advantage that she was also an accomplished painter; and it may be said of her that she specialized largely in Cupids of a delightful chunkiness and ending in a solid base, like that which forms the seemly Finis to this volume. Children were another favourite subject with her, and in 1796 " The Birthday Gift or The Joy of a New Doll," was published. These pleasant stipple engravings, with no special resemblance to silhouette, were described as " from Papers cut by a Lady," but there was no secret made as to their authorship and they were dedicated to Princess Amelia. The publisher of the volume was Tomkins of Bond Street, who—further to illustrate the thesis of this chapter—had in the previous year issued " The Birth and Triumphs of Cupid, from Papers cut by Lady Dashwood." The late Lady Dorothy Nevill owned a priceless album of silhouettes cut or painted by the Princess, with many portraits of her Royal parents in it.

It is, in fact, in albums that Cupid and amateurs alike may be found at their best.

Whenever any wise collector sees or hears of a man mad about any other form of hobby than his own, he says to himself, " There, but for the grace of God knows what, go I " ; and so it is with me about scrap albums. Give me the space and I confess that I could revel in them. I should not limit my ambitions with such gems as those possessed by Mr. Wellesley, Lavater's own tome of heads in silhouette and the delicious Schatzmann book of portraits

(1779–1789) within their printed borders ; I should not even stop short at such quaint *libri amicorum* as that of the Parry family in 1840, with languid ladies painted on settees by Beaumont ; I should not keep to books of merit, nor even bind myself to silhouette ; nothing at all should be too humble or too bad for me so long as it was individual, for if a man notoriously puts half his soul into a first novel, he sticks the whole of it into his scrap-book.

But back to our shadows. . . .

Of the fancy-subject albums, I have seen none more charming than that owned by the Honourable Miss Frances Talbot and made by a rustic kinswoman, Laura MacKenzie, ninety years ago. Fashions changed slow away from London, in those coach-carried days, and they are thus willowy people with all the charm of a century then past who comb their hair or bathe their babies in this splendid scrap-book. It is all cut-paper, several designs upon a page, and every possible domestic scene is represented that could give delight. In one, delightfully Gilbertian, the elders play quietly at chess, whilst in a corner the younger generation has a game of—cards ! One of Miss MacKenzie's beautiful cuttings, to be recognized beyond mistake by furniture and faces no less than by style of cutting, came to me by some devious route in a London shop, and it is reproduced upon plate xxv; a little problem in categories for such as make distinction between silhouette groups and "cut-paper." But in her book, as always, Cupid is supreme. Again and again, beneath trees cut with masterly precision, he is at his games. There he is burning vast sackfuls of hearts in a great cauldron, or—what need for ceremonial?—on a bonfire direct; and when the charming damsel sits at an old-world table to write to her swain, Cupid is up at once upon the chair-back with his bow and shoots her down without remorse.

Yet when I think of Cupid, Silhouette, and scrap-books, my mind leaps to a most piquant contrast: two which stand side by side in the small number of albums that I allow myself.

One is of a glory I despair about setting upon paper. Genteelly small, not half a foot across, it has end-papers of a perfect mauve; its chaste morocco cover, glorious scarlet elaborately tooled with gold, is by a binder "Opposite the Palace"; one cutting only is gummed on to each alternate gilt-edged page; and in it stands the coroneted bookplate of Marguerite, Countess of Blessington.

No need to labour this. The point is clear. Imagine for yourselves the utterly polite ennui with which her ladyship's guests would survey her latest cuttings and pass it on indulgently with a just murmured, " Very pretty, dear. . . ." And pretty, too, they are ; cut in a dozen different colours, touched in cleverely with ink, and shaded off more than once towards the base with a dark water-colour. Dainty maidens saluted by wonderful gallants with cocked hat under arm ; rustic swains that dally under trees ; harlequin up to his merry pranks ; children, of course, at their work and play ; languid youths reclining at angles on Récamier settees ; priceless officers mocking a no less immaculate civilian or bursting into a hot-blooded duel upon the next page to scenes of sugary domestic bliss : it is all very pretty, thoroughly accomplished, and above everything genteel.

The other—what a sad figure it cuts by comparison ! Younger by many years, it yet looks old and gloomy in its stamped black cover with the one gold touch of " Album." The end-papers are of unconvincing yellow. There is no binder's name, no bookplate. But all this is redeemed, when one begins to turn the pages, for here is the love-epic of

THE HAPPY FAMILY.

Cut by Laura Mackenzie, about 1810.

xxv.

an honest sailor. Silhouettes of David Thomson himself, his messmates on the good ship *Griffon*, but more especially of Mary : these are what fill the book—and poems.

David was a poet. True, he did other things. I am afraid he drank sometimes. He wrote indeed not a few poems on that subject. " But first, I should say to inspire me " (he writes in '41, when he was at the hot-blood age of twenty), " I took up a bumper of hot," and ends his poem, written in dejection caused by absence, with this significant admission :

> " *But not being much of a grumbler,*
> *I thought it was better to stop,*
> *So next time I took up the tumbler,*
> *I finished it—every drop* "—

an easy enough way of ending inconvenient inspiration. Three years later, in any case, David is convinced—it may be by his liver—that drink was a mistake, and writes a lyric finely entitled " Wine Should be Used like Medicine." This is dated at sea, January '44 ; but one may see that David kept a broad mind still, for verse four of a March poem lays down about the teetotal convert like himself :

> *" Besides, he gets so very thin,*
> *Though his appetite's prodigious,*
> *His bones come almost through his skin,*
> *And then he's so religious."*

It is, therefore, with a certain horror that we see
his June verses to be entitled: " The Amusement of
Drinking. . . ." But I think there was no relapse,
for this, the last reference to the topic, ends :

> *" And if we don't our talents improve*
> *(If it's true what the Bible tells us)*
> *Our souls will go at their next remove*
> *Wherever the Devil compels us."*

No, we can pass on with an easy mind to the idyll.
Mary was a pretty girl, exactly his own age. She
was, in fact, a very pretty girl ; many silhouettes
bear witness to that fact, but more especially one
touched with gold ; and the heart of David, himself
no beauty, beat wisely true to her. At least, I
think it did. Certainly there is a poem to Lucy,
but of a venial nature. There is equally that other
to a lady unnamed, who on his travels has asked
for a poem and gets one which ends, " I think in
reward of my pains you should certainly give me a

kiss." And yet more flagrantly in need of explanation are the lines to Elizabeth in 1830, Elizabeth whom he first met "Upon a fine autumnal eve," what mystic time "The moon was up, the sun retiring," out at Beaumont Hill:

> " *Since that time I often in fancy behold*
> *The valley on which I there gazed with thee.*
> *I am almost sure that I hear thy voice*
> *And see thy lovely form beside me. . . .*"

Well, sailors are notoriously licensed as to that, and after all, it is not till next year that he writes to Mary:

> " *And in the visions of the night*
> *Thy form alone I see.*"

Also a later David, revising the verses to Elizabeth, has recanted with his own hand—or is it a forgery by Mary's?—and changed that word "lovely" to the less bard-like "dumpy."

And after all, you must read this album backwards, like a Chinee or woman, if you would get its proper ending; for inside the front cover, opposite two profiles of the young lovers gazing in each other's eyes, there is written simply, yet who can guess with how much pride :

> " *To Mary,*
> *from her Husband,*
> *D. Thomson.*"

VII
LABELS

CHAPTER VII

LABELS

LABELS may sound a dull and unprofitable subject, yet in them lies great magic for the silhouette collector.

Imagine for an instant—*parvis componere magna*—that the great artists or great miniaturists of the eighteenth century had placed behind their work a printed account of what they thought the chief merit of their peculiar styles ! Right or wrong (and seldom indeed is the artist a critic . . . of his own creations), such an opinion would be valued above gold by any decent-thinking connoisseur.

And this, in effect, is what was done by these dear, simple, enthusiasts in the new Art of Silhouette. Full of wondrous words to express the full mystery and importance of what arrived in England with all the decorous prestige of a classical accomplishment, they pressed into a few printed words delicious synopses of their skill, which have the rare though often advertised distinction of being both instructive and amusing. If few things could be more charming than Master Hubard, with his wooden-looking cutouts, describing himself solemnly as " Papyrotomist," or Haines (of the Chain Pier) as a " Scissorgraphist," yet nothing at all could be more useful than that Rosenberg, that master of cold outline, should describe himself as deliberately working " in imitation of stone." That one phrase, which seems more and more inspired to anyone who studies the Bath artist's work, raises to a virtue the lack of softness in it which easily might otherwise have seemed a vice.

Moreover, even optimists have never denied the claim of this world to be wicked, and already there appear on all sides forgeries of an increasing merit. They are getting their eye set, these fakers ; the day of the rought cut-out will soon pass : specimens on chalk " by " Miers, on glass " by " Rosenberg, will trickle, I feel confident, ere long into the London shops. Already one great antique gallery has sent forth the pronouncement that no more specimens will be bought without labels. These little printed papers are going to become, in the new vogue of Silhouette, what " marks " have been in the old-china craze. They will be forged, no doubt, in time ;

136

A LADY,

Painted on card by Mrs. Beetham.

but cost apart, this is a bigger enterprise than skilful copying of a black head on chalk. Labels and old frames—these are the fatal snags that lie in the poor forger's track; and these must be no less the quarry set before all intelligent silhouette collectors.

It is very well worth while, then, before proceeding to the later humours of the Label, to consider those used by the first great silhouettists and see, as preachers say, what can be learnt from them.

First lesson of all, perhaps; that as with curio-dealers, so it was with silhouettists. The most superior put least in their shop window.

Mrs. Beetham was the very essence of superiority. No need to look further than her dainty ladies and ineffably genteel young men, the plain distinction of her rose-wood frames, the costly splendour of her gold and cream domed glasses, the decorous white chalk behind. Had she but lived in this era of hotels and cinemas, she must have called her portraits likenesses *de luxe!* And as the last touch of superiority, desolating surely to her rivals, she placed upon her engraved label merely these words :

" Profiles
in
Miniature
by
Mrs. Beetham,
No. 27
Fleet Street.
1785."

These severe words were engraved amid a wealth
of flourishes recalling a different art, Calligraphy,
and dots forecasting Beardsley. At the four corners
are small heads in profile ; but on oval frames or
actual miniatures these were naturally sacrificed by
a ruthless snip from the scissors she no doubt
despised.

Unluckily, that " 1785 " must not encourage
owners to believe they have the very date of their
pet specimens : it merely marks the printing of her
plate and occurs on all the labels I have ever found
of Mrs. Beetham at the summit of her fame.

Even the best of us, however, have our pasts ; and
Mrs. Beetham, before she reached this glory of plaster
and gilt glasses, plied a humbler trade with portraits
painted upon card and even cut from paper. Three

specimens in my possession, two beaux and a belle, are delicately cut, ruffle and periwig in open-work; the black is seemingly applied with soot on a white surface, to be gently handled; details of hair or dress are touched in lightly with a pencil, scarcely to be noticed till the glass is removed; whilst each bust ends in that jagged line to which I have already called attention in the more ambitious Beethams (pl. iv). Upon the back of one beau and the belle *Page 30.* is a most curious label, too big—alas!—for the small pear-wood oval, so that much of it is lost. Enough remains, however, to prove it as Mrs. Beetham's, and lest any doubt should linger as to whether back-boards and frames had not belonged to some quite different silhouettes, old Sol—kindest of friends to the collectors and worst foe to the dark-loving faker—burning his way patiently through the thin paper has left flawless profiles on the wooden backing.

Behind these quite indubitable Beethams, then, is found this fragment of a label:

(? By *ap*)*plication*, leagued with good *nat*(*ural* gifts ?)

(MRS.) BEETHA(M).

(has ena)bled herself to remedy a *Dificulty*, much

139

lamen(ted and)

universally experienced, by

PARENTS, LOVERS, AND FRIENDS,

The former, assisted by *her* ART *may see their off-
spring in any part of the terraqueous Globe ;*

Nor can Death obliterate the Featuers from their
fond Remembrance.

LOVERS, the POETS have advanced,

" *Can waft a Sigh from Indus to the Pole.*"

She will graitfy them with more *substantial,* though
ideal

(inter)course by placing the beloved Object to their
view.

FRIENDSHIP is truly valuable, was ever held a
Max(im)

They who deny it never tasted its delicious Fruit.

or shed a Sympathizing Tear.

. . . that was so ENDEARING, nay RAVISHING. . .

. . . separations existed . . ."

MRS. BEETHAM will call into B (eing ?) . . .

(*Cœtera,* as the learned say, *desunt :* and not to
be outdone in Classicism, I shall add : *eheu !*)

LABELS

Here is a very different Mrs. Beetham from that austere lady who printed her new label in 1785! These lines which—but for their spelling—recall the lyric grandeur of a world-famed fruit salt advertisement, no doubt mark a period before the day when Mrs. Beetham, woman and sentimentalist, merged herself into Mrs. Beetham, artist and mere painter of " Profiles in miniature. . . ."

Rosenberg, whose classical restraint would certainly have led one to expect an equal reticence, was luckily (as I have said) far more confiding even in his prime, and his trade-label, found behind all the instances in my collection, is quite a work of art. On top the Royal Arms ; at bottom a scroll with emblems armorial and masonic ; and in the middle, framed within an oval wreathed by flowers :

By Their Majesties' Authority.

MR. ROSENBERG

OF BATH

PROFILE PAINTER

To their Majesties and Royal Family, Begs leave to inform the Nobility and Gentry that he takes most striking like-

nesses in Profile, which he Paints on Glass
in imitation of Stone that will never fade.

Time of sitting one Minute.

Price from 7s. 6d. to £1 1s. 0d. Family
Pieces whole lengths in various Attitudes.

N.B. Likenesses for Rings, Lockets,
Trinkets, and Snuff Boxes."

Time—price—varieties—method—and artistic aim
—Rosenberg is indeed the man for silhouette collectors ; and with it all there is no loss of dignity.

Perhaps, of the bigger men, Miers allowed himself
most freedom as to trumpet-blowing. Upon his
Leeds label—a rarity that gives a thrill indeed, when
found, to the collector—there appear, severely
printed in an oval, these words :

" Perfect likenefses in miniature profile
taken by J. MIERS, LEEDS, and reduced
on a plan entirely new, which preserves the
most exact Symmetry and animated exprefsion of the Features much superior to
any other method. Time of sitting one
Minute. N.B. He keeps the original
Shades, and can supply those he has once

FRAMED MINIATURES ON IVORY

Signed, or labelled, 1 and 2 by Miers ; 3 by Mrs. Beetham. Actual size.

taken with any number of Copies. Those who have shades by them may have them reduced to any size and drefsed in the present Taste."

This final inducement to the unwilling middle-aged was also offered (be it noted) by a contemporary Liverpool artist, Mrs. Lightfoot, an artist very similar to Miers in method as in label : and was, indeed, more to be looked for from female subtlety. It is of interest to note the word " taken," coolly appropriated later by photography from its defeated rival ; also the word " Shade," which I should like to see revived in place of the alien and unhistoric " Silhouette."

Beneath the oval there is seen this more modest postscript :

" Orders (at any Time) addressed to him at LEEDS in Yorkshire, will be punctually dispatched."

On a portrait of Burns' mother in the Wellesley collection, Miers' address is given as " Lowerhead Row, Leeds." Although this might seem to point to an earlier address, it marks more probably a date at which the profilist's fame had not spread even across his own native city. Later, one does not doubt, his thronged studio came to rank with the glories of Leeds.

When Miers grew yet more famous and moved to London, he increased the time of sitting to three minutes and on the whole became less self-assertive, for on his later specimens he merely claims to execute " Likenesses in Profile in a style of superior excellence with unequalled accuracy, which convey the most forcible exprefsion and animated character even in the very minute size for Rings, Broaches, Lockets, &c. &c." (He is by now " Profile Painter And Jeweller," at 111 Strand, London, " opposite Exeter Change.")

It must at the same time be admitted that, speaking broadly, the London Miers is not such fine work as the Leeds, if more elaborate and, in his later years, commonly adorned with gold. No doubt, like all silhouettists and some artists, he had, as his circle grew, to bring into his studio " shades " of another sort, and perhaps many a signed Miers (or anyhow many a labelled Miers) has little enough else to do with his own hand. On a fine woman's head, painted in black on chalk with charming softness in the hair and dress, framed with the pomp of a black and gold glass—" a beautiful Miers," many an expert

has said, seeing it on my walls—there is a label
thus :

"THOMAS LOVELL,

from Mr. Miers,

PROFILE-PAINTER, JEWELLER, AND MINIATURE
FRAME MAKER,

32 Bread Street, Cheapside, London,
Engages to take Likenesses in Profile to
reduce and copy old Shades or Sketches
for Rings, Lockets, Frames, &c. &c.
N.B. By preserving the original Draught
he can supply Duplicates without an after
Sitting.

Mourning Rings and every article in the
Jewellery line."

This is the only Lovell label I have ever seen, nor
does the name occur in Mrs. Jackson's list of silhouettists, but it is utterly beyond dispute ; and how
many shades by Lovell may not be masquerading
still as Miers' ? Perhaps there were other assistants,
too, who never blossomed out as being "from Mr.
Miers." And soon he had taken into partnership, was proud to own it on his labels, Field, who
when working alone, described himself on a minute

oblong as merely : " Profile Painter, Jeweller, Seal Engraver, &c., No. 2 Strand, near Charing Cross," but added " To their Majesties, By Appointment." Field mainly worked in black and gold, or black and brown, frequently on card, and often signed underneath the bust. Upon the death of Miers, he embarked again, with a much fuller label that owed a little possibly to his late partner, though he reduced the time of sitting, which latterly had been five minutes, to the old mid-period three.

It would be tedious to quote further. Charles had a label—none too modest ; " the first profilist in England "—but used it all too little. That of another silhouettist is sufficiently curious to claim some few lines more before I pass to the Victorian excesses. Upon the silhouette of a girl, the Honourable C. Massy, roughly executed upon chalk, an oval label with a decorative design bears the words, amongst others : ". . . preserves ye most exact Symmetry and animated Exprefsion of ye Features superior to any other Method. . . . Reduces old Ones and drefses them in ye present TASTE. . . . Set in elegant gilt frames at 6s. 6d. only."

This archaic adapter of Miers' label worked in a method largely similar, though with less delicacy,

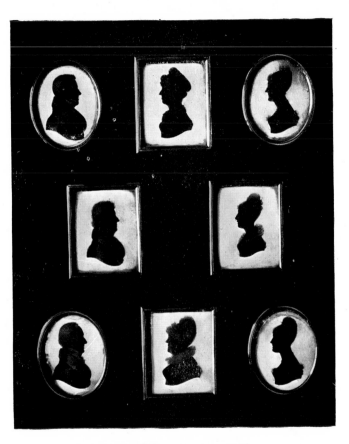

A FAMILY, assigned to Field.
(Showing the large papier-maché frame.)

bore the name **I. Thomason,** and practised at **33**
Caple Street, Dublin. He was certainly working
at an early date; describes himself in a newspaper
announcement of 1790 period as "from England";
and it is idle by now to dispute whether he or Miers
first evolved their common self-laudation. Rought
of the Cornmarket, Oxford, another eighteenth-
century exponent, backed his perruqued under-
graduates (painted on glass in stern lines and a
curiously deep black paint) with a design that would
not have shamed Bartolozzi. Torond of 18 Wells
Street boasted rightly to work "in the genteellest
taste." This very happily expresses the gentle
charm of several specimens that are among my dearest
treasures. In fact, these earlier advertisements
would form an interesting collection in themselves,
for anybody heartless enough to turn the silhouettes
face inward to the wall. . . .

It was, however, the Victorians who reduced labels
to their highest pitch—and their lowest absurdity.

Edouart, however puny he may look beside his
great predecessors, towered above the small men of
his day; and in accordance with the shop-window
canon his label has a certain dignified reserve, as
thus:

" Likenesses in Profile, Executed by Mons.
EDOUART, Who begs to observe that his Likenesses are produced by the Scissors alone,
and are preferable to any taken by Machines,
inasmuch as by the above method the expression of the Passions, and peculiarities of
Character, are brought into action, in a style
which has not hitherto been attempted by
any other artist. Numerous Proof Specimens may be seen at Mrs. Bays's, Trinity
Street, Cambridge.

Full length—5s. 0d. Ditto, children under
8 years of age—3s. 6d. Profile Bust—2s. 0d.

Attendance abroad, double, if not more
than two Full Length Likenesses are
taken.

Any additional Cutting, as Instrument,
Table, &c. &c. to be paid accordingly."

The last item is instructive. With it in mind, one
tends—on looking round a wall of Edouarts—to rate
the all too often unnamed sitters by the amount of
furniture around them. That young man, who
always until now had been a favourite, stands forth
in this new snobbish light as a mere tyro shivering
upon life's bottom rung, and painfully unable to

PLate xxix

MR. STERN AT THE SPINET

Painted by Torond

afford (tempt Edouart never so wisely) table or instrument or even his own hat in hand. . . . And that old gentleman, who always seemed so dull and podgy, gains fresh importance, for behold he sits (an extra, this we know from Edouart's own book) upon a chair with table, three books, top-hat, and a vase before him, whilst (down on your hams, ye snobs !) the curtained window, with seascape complete, is no less than hand-painted !

As to the cost of this last no label that I have yet found will throw any light. Other facts emerge from some : a bust was frequently one shilling only (possibly in poorer towns than Cambridge, or those with less gilt youth about), and duplicates were roughly at half-price ; but nowhere can one learn exactly how much Dives spent on his hand-painted room, what poor young Lazarus had saved by standing chastely on a chill white card, or the precise social and financial position of those who vaunted themselves in a stiff lithographed apartment.

On the back of a silhouette that shows a girl beside a large stone vase (no doubt an " instrument " and " paid accordingly," in the grim formula), and in front of a lithographed terrace with a river-prospect, there is a very interesting label. It was, in fact, for this that I bought the specimen, which is in

Edouart's worst manner. This last fact has not deterred him from both signing and adding an imposing label in circular form. At top there stands in silhouette the Royal Arms, at bottom a portrait of the King with crown and olive-wreath, whilst up the two curves run extended scissors, which look at first sight much more like so many pairs of spectacles. Amid all this, at various angles, may be found :

" Taken with scissors only.
Silhouette likenesses under the Special Patronage of H.R.H. the Duke of Gloucester.

MONSIEUR EDOUART.

Full Length Standing	5.0.	Duplicates	3.0.
do. Sitting	7.0.	do.	4.0.
Children under 8 years of age	3.6.	do.	2.6.
Busts	2.6.	do.	1.6.

Full lengths taken from busts,
or description of absent or deceased persons.

The likenesses taken in Five Minutes.

Frames at Manufacturers' Prices.

Orders sent, with Cash for the amount, Post Paid, to Mr. John Mc. Rae, 155 Cheapside, London, Agent to Mons. E., will be attended to immediately."

150

And underneath the royal bust appears : " Silhouettes of Celebrated Characters, 3s. each." This, I have said, is informative, as it explains the countless duplicates of Dr. Simeon and other popular divines. Another sentence, " Taken with the scissors only," may be tardily commended to such dealers as have in their extensive showrooms painted or gilt specimens " by " Monsieur Edouart. . . . It is to be remarked in passing that Edouart, having grown from Mons. to Monsieur and got a London agent, to say nothing of a royal patron, has sensibly increased his prices ; and the fact that the silhouette in front of all this pomp is feeble must not encourage to an easy cynicism. Let us pronounce it a coincidence . . . or say that Edouart, like Rosenberg, was at his best with males ; the penalty in each case of a method so severe.

Edouart probably obtained the highest fees at this time, although, of course, the earlier masters had received far more and even then got much less than their foreign rivals.

Certainly Master Hubard, who was cutting in the twenties, made no extravagant demands, so far as money went. " A strikingly correct likeness," he assures his patrons, " with a frame and a glass, for one shilling, can invariably be relied on at the Hubard Gallery."

So far, so good ; but one must not place too much reliance on the later statements of this label, which is found behind a full-length portrait of James Lee, a middle-aged man in full riding kit ; possibly a coachman and offered to me (like many others) as a Wellington :

> " The curious and much admired Art of cutting out likenesses with common scissors (without drawing or machine) originated in this establishment in 1822. Master Hubard was the first youth known to possess the extraordinary talent of delineating Profile Likenesses with Scissors, and his works, consisting of Military, Architectural, and other subjects, are still considered the finest specimens of the Papyrotomic art.
>
> As the originator of this New and Curious Art, Master Hubard was in 1823 presented with an expensive silver Palette by the Glasgow Philosophical Society, and by that Society his Exhibition was first designated the HUBARD GALLERY.

LABELS

As the 'Nursery of Extraordinary Juvenile Talent,' the Hubard Gallery has since been universally known in all the principal towns in Gt. Britain, Ireland, the United States, and the Canadas."

It would be presumptuous, no less than useless, to cross swords at this time of day with the Glasgow Philosophical Society (which anyhow had quite a pretty taste in names); but if Master Hubard originated cut-paper portraits in 1822, there does arise a quite philosophic doubt, which even the G.P.S. need not have despised, about explaining the countless earlier examples. Perhaps it was this feeling that caused the lad (who must soon have grown into a Company, one would suppose, so many specimens did he produce) to use this high-flown label seldom and be content with a mere stamp-relief, " taken at the Hubard Gallery," or sometimes even the two last words alone. This is a big drop from the earliest days of all where his silhouettes were " cut with common scissors without drawing or machine by the celebrated Little Boy, Master Hubard."

Master Hubard's claim, however, was quite in

accordance with the spirit of his age. Any silhouettist who hid his light beneath a bushel might have got snugly underneath with it, himself as well, for all the good that he would do. Already the proud " artist " was sinking to a loud-voiced showman. Soon his " Gallery " would be a draught-swept shanty on a pier. . . .

Meanwhile, therefore, Skeolan must warn all and sundry that he was making a " short stay "; announce that his profiles were " faithful, elegant, and characteristic " (this at the back of a most wooden group); " the best ever seen in Halifax "— no less; and drop only at the end to saying that " accuracy " would be guaranteed; Haines must practise his " scissorgraphy "; Gapp (also of the Chain Pier) make it obvious that he has " no connection with any other person," is in the " Third Tower," and will there (apparently) do " Ladies and Gentlemen on Horseback, 7s. 6d.," " Single Horses, 5s.," or " Dogs, 1s. 6d.," all likenesses being " most wonderful "; whilst Liverpool, never to be left behind, produces Dempsey who reminds " Emigrants, Travellers, and the Public," that the new penny postage " offers a safe and cheap method " of sending mementoes, which he is willing to supply on terms the moderateness of which clearly causes him a pain to be worked off only by a crescendo of exclamation marks : " Likenesses in shade, 3*d*. ! Bronzed, 6*d*. ! ! Coloured, 1*s*. 6*d*. ! ! ! " Alas ! there is (without the exclamation marks) that most significant of notices : " And upwards " : a postscript still familiar on trays of curios "All at Five Shillings."

Well, they are dead now, all these dear simple men ; nothing is left of them except the shadows that they cut and their pretentious claims ; but they all did their best, leaving behind them much that was curious or good, nothing—no man of them—that could do harm to anyone ; and may we other artists have no less to claim when we make up our labels for our life-time's judgment !

VIII

SOME COLLECTIONS

CHAPTER VIII

SOME COLLECTIONS

It is commonly admitted that whilst envy in itself must be ranged among the vices, it leads the way to enterprise, ambition, energy and other virtues. Perhaps therefore I am ethically justified in taking my public a brief tour around some of the most notable collections.

Every one knows the State Rooms at Knole, that wonderful mansion which clutches greedily the wealth of a dozen museums in its old rambling galleries : peerless corridors of Jacobean furniture ; pictures by Lely, Reynolds, Gainsborough ; needle-work, carving, silver ; everything beautiful that the industrious past has handed down to its most favoured children : but few are possibly aware that in the great house's private wing there is one room devoted solely to a more modern art, the art of Silhouette. This is the home of Lady Sackville's own collection ; partly inherited, partly bought, partly given by kind or less appreciative friends.

THE ART OF SILHOUETTE

The room may be described as a harmony in black and white. Everywhere are silhouettes: pictures, ornaments, and china. On the jugs and basins is an effective pattern introducing medallion silhouettes, wherein I seemed to recognize Queen Alexandra, Lord and Lady Sackville themselves, together with two ancestresses, the Duchess of Bedford and Countess of Derby, whose profiles are adapted from authentic silhouettes now hanging on the walls. When the room is occupied by any visitor there is brought in a morning tea-service of the same unique design, whilst even paper-stand and blotter bear fine-cut subject silhouettes, which I think from their style may safely be attributed to Wilhelm Müller. The whole room is an original idea superbly carried out.

As to the collection proper, pressed for a single adjective I should describe it above all things as uncommon. By this I must not be read to mean that it is in any way a freak collection, but rather that whilst keeping to silhouettes of quality and value it yet steers free of all the most familiar names. It may be that there are specimens by Mrs. Beetham, Rosenberg, and Miers; one Edouart I certainly remember; but for the most part I recall it as a

A POPE (PIUS VI.) AND A SOLDIER

By Foster (Signed).

fascinating gallery of gems to which, off-hand, one would be hard pressed to set an artist's name. Some splendid specimens in black and gold stand gaily out in a sidelight, one signed " Coog, 1789," another showing a black portrait on gold set within a silver urn. This is unsigned but bears the legend, " Pensez à moi, 1812." A few Continental portraits in printed borders, one signed " fait par Joubert, peintre en miniature," catch the eye by their bold outlines. Others, English, attract no less by reason of their delicacy. Quite the most charming and unusual of these last is the large full-length portrait of " the last Lord Fauconberg." Beneath a looped curtain there sits reading a perruqued young man in uniform. Table, chair, ink-pot, everything is as perfect and distinguished as himself. His cocked hat lies before him on the table, and gazing up at him in helpless adoration is a depressed hound, apparently conscious of being the least well-bred thing in the tableau. This beautiful specimen of a full-length figure-study is signed by Wellings, who worked in England around 1785 but was not always so happy in his work as here. Specimens by Foster or Spornberg, even red-coat soldiers, however representative, lose a little of their glamour beside anything so beyond the usual as this or as the delicious advertisement of a silhouettist which hangs beside the bed. Three women and a man, their hair dressed in the style of somewhere around 1800, fill oval niches in a black square whereon is inscribed, "Profiles taken here at 2. 6. each."

But it is time now to look at the china, a department in which Lady Sackville may rate her collection almost peerless. The pen of a china-expert would be needed to describe properly the vases, tea-cups, bowls, nor do these specimens fall strictly in my scope for they display another art. One thing, however, is of interest here: the freedom with which George III appears. George was of course a glutton for silhouette, and here we have him upon stately Worcester vases over a foot high, bearing such legends as "An honest man's the noblest work of God," and also upon smaller mugs with much less flowery mottoes. One of these, still seen about in shops, seems almost modern in its familiar laconism: "Happy Jubilee, 1809. . . ." This is different indeed from the Shakespearian inscription underneath another portrait of his Majesty in Lady Sackville's silhouette room :

" *May he live,*
Longer than I have time to tell his Years !
Ever belov'd, and loving, may his rule be !
And when old Time shall lead him to his end,
Goodness and he fill up one Monument ! "

But far the most pleasant memorial to George III
at Knole is in another place. Up in the George III
room, hangs a curiously interesting silhouette of
both the King and Queen. They face each other,
white busts engraved on a small mirror. This is the
work of " Mr. John Pye, apprentice, born 1753," and
very fine it is. Sometimes, I think John Pye must
wish that it might take its chance among the shadows
in that other room.

Mrs. Bromley Taylor is another collector who has,
so to speak, concentrated upon Silhouette, but in her
case it is a London drawing-room that is the shrine
of shadows. Cleverly arranged, with smaller frames
grouped round the long full-lengths, and one wall
varying the scheme by beautiful Lucas wax-heads,
the room is effective, individual, and suprisingly
free from any suspicion of freakish eccentricity.
Convincingly natural, it fills the first duty of any
room by expressing the owner's personality. Mrs.

Bromley Taylor is a real enthusiast on Silhouette and one of the pioneers in that collection. She has bought always more with the eye of an artist than with the sordid back-thought of a connoisseur, and if this has perhaps limited the value of her collection, it has probably increased its charm. Names and labels, what are they, to any normal mind, beside a grace of decoration? Mrs. Bromley Taylor has some splendid specimens by Miers, Foster, and the other masters, but she has bought them for themselves, not for the names they bear, and who shall say that she is wrong? Certainly there is no name or label on the choicest of her miniatures, tiny profile heads of Napoleon and Josephine, black and gold on glass, surrounded by an ornamental border, but only a museum pedant could think worse of it for that.

Personally, though I cannot deny the effectiveness and charm of these two black-and-white rooms, I confess that I best love my silhouettes in a stiff line above the mellow gold of an old mirror, or hung in a festoon round colour-print and pastel. Picture and silhouette both seem to gain new value from their contrast. And when—as happens—the ever-increasing profiles begin to give the walls an oddly chicken-pox appearance, here is an expedient that

I believe original and know from my experience to be effective. Take an old mirror (for this is no less than a recipe) of the long, low-lying sort known as a three-decker—one of those dim gold affairs, a large glass in the centre flanked by smaller glasses at the sides, with ever so respectable gilt balls beneath the overhanging eave—and heartlessly remove the glasses. Now in their place fix three wood panels covered with velvet of a restful, ancient-seeming green. The thing sounds horrible, the desolation of Victorian abomination ; but when small silhouettes, especially the early ones in oval frames of brass, are hung within the panels tactfully, believe me the effect is charming. A centre-piece has come for the collection, and the walls meanwhile are ridded of their plague of spots.

No such expedient can help the silhouette collector who works upon the scale of Mr. Francis Wellesley, but he has grappled happily with this aspect of his wonderful collection. True, in the drawing-room of his Surrey home there is a bulky chest full to its limit with specimens that other connoisseurs might struggle to possess, beautiful signed specimens in fine frames lumbered pell-mell without any order ; but those thought worthy to be shown are most effectively displayed. To the countless people who believe silhouettes to be black cut-paper portraits in Victorian frames, Mr. Wellesley's dining-room might prove an almost dangerous shock. Nothing more handsome, nothing finer, can well be imagined than the massed effect of black and gold in the silhouette trophies (for I can find no better word) that Mr. Wellesley has hung between his beautiful old oils. Nothing is admitted here but what its artist thought worthy of a gilt-glass setting. Specimens by Miers or by Mrs. Beetham, gems every one, are hung in great bunches that might be expected to kill their individual worth, but actually succeed in lending value to each other. Not in the whole room is there one cut silhouette, all is chalk or glass; and here it was that the Victoria and Albert Museum made the greatest inroad when Mr. Wellesley promised lately to loan a part of this collection, which he and his wife, equally enthusiastic, have gathered together from almost every part of Europe.

Next door, in the smoking-room, silhouette holds its own amply with the wonderful early plumbago drawings, which are Mr. Wellesley's new hobby, even with his marvellous show of miniatures by all of the accepted masters; but this is not surprising,

Plate xxxi

WILLIAM PITT, 1788

In black and gold, on glass, by Fepk.

(In the possession of Francis Wellesley, Esq.)

xxxi.

for here again are no late Georgians or Victorians, nothing but fine specimens by Rosenberg and his compeers, fine instances of all the Continental profilists, together with such curious examples as have already been referred to in these pages. This comes close indeed to being a room of pure silhouette, but it is restful to the eye as well as being a delight to the collector's soul. All over the house, indeed, one may find traces of the hobby, though Mr. Wellesley is of course a man by no means of one fixed idea. That a connoisseur of such world-famous taste should have relapsed on Silhouette is in itself indeed sufficient answer to those who sniff contempt at the whole art of shadows. Enough to say that Mr. Wellesley's most cherished Downman, his most priceless miniature, does not seem out of keeping with, or any way superior to, the choicest of his silhouettes. The whole place is an harmonious treasure-house.

In the drawing-room no silhouettes are hung, so far as I remember, but china keeps up the tradition— Worcester tributes to George similar to those at Knole ("More dear to his subjects," "Mercy and Truth preserve the King ") ; Meissen china in black, gold and blue ; Dresden, showing Goethe and his circle, black, gold, green, and blue ; Furstenburg plaques, kings and princesses dated 1786, surrounded by gold rims—whilst in a glass-faced cabinet is arranged his gallery of jewelled miniatures in silhouette. Here, often in the rarest settings, you may see tiny gems by Mrs. Beetham, Rosenberg, and Miers ; double lockets breathing their romance ; patch-boxes with the shadow of their owner on them ; Smart the miniaturist painted by Mrs. Beetham ; curious red miniatures by Spornberg ; a Field on ivory, the smallest silhouette to be possibly imagined ; rings holding women with a coloured dress, and innumerable perfect specimens by continental artists.

So far as connoisseurs go, " seldom comes glory till a man be dead." Mention silhouettes, the average dealer and most auction-goers will refer to the late Montague Guest and his historic sale at Christie's. But when the Francis Wellesley sale comes—long hence may it be !—a sleepy world will rub its eyes to find that a greater connoisseur has all the while been in their midst. Mr. Wellesley cannot perhaps claim to have been among the first of silhouette collectors, but he has made himself the greatest. Almost all the Guest collection is at Westfield, and forms a very small part of a far greater whole. Mr. Wellesley, as though he felt that his silhouette collection had reached its zenith, has lately published a luxurious volume of "One Hundred Silhouette Portraits selected from the Collection of Francis Wellesley," with a preface by Weymer Mills. Only a hundred copies of this book, beautifully printed by the University Press, Oxford, have been issued, and these will repose largely in the principal museums. No finer catalogue of silhouettes is ever likely to be published, and I think myself very fortunate indeed to be, by Mr. Wellesley's generous thought, the owner of what must always rank among the rarest of treasures for future silhouette-collectors, nor less to be allowed the use of some blocks from the catalogue.

Lest the bare mention of so many gems beyond their reach should depress the neophytes no less than sauntering through a museum, I may possibly stretch the title of this chapter to include a few hints on "What to Collect."

Mr. Wellesley, be it said at once, is in the eighteenth century, or not much after. He scorns Victorians or late Georgians, and this is a field therefore easy of access to later or less favoured connoisseurs.

One might in fact draw up a rising scale for any would-be silhouette collector. First and lowest would come (in the glorious vernacular) *any* old black thing. Those with no higher ambition should first, however, read the passage upon forgeries in a later chapter.

Secondly, we should attack signed or labelled late Georgians and Victorians : Master Hubard, Frith, Field, Hervé, Beaumont and their kidney ; with Edouart and Foster as our highest good. This should still be an easy collection for anyone with energy and time.

Next in the rising scale would come eighteenth century unsigned. Here the perruque or piled head-dress would serve as our hall-mark.

Lastly, for those of overpowering ambition, the eighteenth century, signed, labelled, and in the authentic frames. Miers, Rosenberg, Mrs. Beetham, Spornberg, Jorden, Charles, Thomason, and Hamlet —such for the most part will be their narrow list of possibles, unless they branch out into the innumerable artists who worked in Germany, Russia, and France. Such, too, is the hard way that I have set myself in future.

Of course, however, in between these obvious grades we may find possible collections full of interest. Silhouette prints, for instance. A chapter, nay a book, could easily be written about these. Apart from

Plate xxxii

AN OFFICER OF THE GUARDS

Painted on paper in Regimental Colours.

(In the possession of Francis Wellesley, Esq.)

xxxii.

countless prints displaying a sure method of taking
profiles, or all those flabby classic couples who
illustrate in stipple the Origin of Silhouette, there are
delightful frontispieces to innumerable volumes.
Plump Edward Gibbon with his snuff-box (from
his quarto edition, 1796); Dr. Keate with pupil-
terrifying stride; naval captains who had suffered
shipwreck; above all, clergymen who published
sermons—such are but a few of those who accepted
the profilists' offer to provide suitable frontispieces.
Some of these are crude indeed and with delicious
legends. Politicians, again, and popular preachers
attained the fame of separate silhouette prints sold
like mere broadsides. In the Victoria and Albert
Museum Print Room may be seen prints of Lord
Brougham (inscribed, " I see, sir, I see, it comes to
this "), Earl Grey with Reform Bill on table before
him, Lord John Russell and Daniel O'Connell,
published by I. Bruce, who also issued a familiar print
of Wellington, his legs up on a chair. Among frontispieces the palm must go to the beautiful portrait of
Robert Burns by Miers, but the high-water mark
of a purely silhouette-print collection would be in
the fine aquatints issued by Colnaghi. An equestrian
George III, a duplicate of which hangs fittingly in

the Pavilion at Brighton, is inscribed: "This likeness of the most excellent and venerable Majesty
King George III, in the fiftieth year of his reign . . ."
by Charles Rosenberg, engraved by Stadler, October 1,
1810. It is, of course, in colours except for the face.

Some of the best prints would be obtained from
books, and anyone with a stern conscience might prefer
to be a book-collector. Here the rarities would be
Edouart's " Treatise," already described, and such
kindred volumes as Barbara Anne Townshend's " Art
of Cutting out Designs In Black Paper," of which
Mr. Wellesley owns a copy. But others more within
the general reach would be Konewka's " Midsummer
Night's Dream " (Longmans, 1868) or " My Young
Days " ; Albert Smith's " Rasperl " (issuing oddly
from the Egyptian Hall) ; the books with frontispieces above mentioned ; and above all Lavater
in the big quarto edition. The later octavo edition,
published 1789, omits the big plate showing the
method of taking profiles, as also the large full-length
plates, which under initials hide (I believe) Madame
de Staël and George Stubbs, R.A. These in themselves are beautiful, but the comments of Lavater are
still better. From the mere shadow he will dogmatize
on anybody's soul. His kindly delineation of his own

profile in particular must bring refreshment to the weariest mind, and—as a sample of his quality—about the charming silhouette of Mr. Stubbs, R.A., and a boy, he has these naïve remarks :

" Here we are presented with a man arrived at maturity and a most promising youth, though in silhouettes of the whole figure the effect of the light always injures the clearness and accuracy of the profile " (this would shock Edouart), " it will however without hesitation be admitted that the principal figure has a character of wisdom, and that the young man discovers hopeful dispositions. . . . The silhouette of the grown man is much inferior to the object which it represents. . . . The youth . . . will have to combat with caprice and obstinacy. I love him nevertheless with all my soul, though I have never seen him and know nothing of him."

Two pages earlier, having prophesied—from the profile—great things of another youth, whom I suspect to be his son, he ends : " If he disappoint that expectation, farewell to physiognomy."

Lavater's " Physiognomy " is indeed a book that all silhouette collectors must possess. Apart from its generous supply of silhouettes—Frederick of Prussia, the inevitable George, and many other men of note—

it holds a long and charming appreciation of the art from one competent to judge.

A third possible collection (for space demands a bald economy of words and I am tempted to a chapter upon each) would be quite broadly " Paper-work." This ambitious heading would include those subject silhouettes that have been dealt with in another essay ; all such portraits as are actually cut, pin-prick pictures, and those fascinating boxfuls of rolled-paper that hang upon the wall and throw a ray out from the golden edges of their dim elaborate castles—a field wide enough for even the most rabid buyer.

Much more difficult would lie the path before a fourth collector, who should concentrate upon the black and gold glass pictures. First of all the portraits, French or English, profiles in the fullest sense, such as that of Pitt upon pl. xxxi, but then diverging to groups that still might be termed silhouettes (a long array of glorious gold students of astronomy against a dead-black background is signed with the name Belluti), and so on to ambitious subjects having no such possible pretension but getting nearer to the genus of glass picture. This collection, interesting and full of decorative merit,

174

Plate xxxiii

FREDERICK OF PRUSSIA,

Is. Johnson del. Alderton suff.

(Size of original. 15-in. × 12.)

would involve departure from the patriotic stand-point of No Foreigners (always, of course, unless they worked in England!). Two of the finest I have found—fierce hunting scenes with silver hares pursued by golden hawks against a leaden sky—are signed by Rudolph, 1794.

Lastly, for an age that worships the ugly and mistrusts prettiness as inartistic, there might be a freak collection; the oddest items from all the above possible collections. Puzzle-prints, where silhouetted heads of Buonaparte and family are found in violets; Victorian abominations with real clothes upon them; toy-books where the figures move and leave shadows behind, the barrister a parrot but the girl a puss; everything odd that could be bound up with a dainty art. Here the most pleasant items certainly would be such a "mixed" item as the fine portrait of Frederick the Great, pl. xxxiii, half silhouette and half calligraphy, or those shadow-cuts which only throw the silhouette when held between white paper and a concentrated light. Up to the present I have found nobody who could explain the origin or object of these ingenious precursors of the magic lantern. Lady Dorothy Nevill, who must always rank as the first collector of so-called cut-paper, had many fine examples of this curious art, some by Princess Elizabeth, daughter of George III, who had profile-mania in the blood. Lately in a bookshop I bought an early collection at one swoop; many of them copied from such familiar prints as "Comedy" or "Tragedy"; and the effect is quite incredible. No name or date is on them, but some of the portrait subjects—(Napoleon, Britannia weeping over Princess Charlotte's tomb, George IV, Miss Stephens, Kean, Cooke, Mrs. Siddons, Mrs. Egerton as Meg, Mrs. Johnstone in Timour the Tartar, Erskine, Kitty Fisher)—indicate the period sufficiently. The most astounding fact about these shadow-cuts is the effect of roundness which is given to a face or figure. Unhappily there seems no way of framing them to show their merits, nor does a reproduction of the original (pl. xxxiv) give any hint of the shadow's effect though it displays the amazing skill necessitated in the cutter.

I have it in me to hope that, even if some are urged to start on shadow-cuts (they may see some of average quality in the Victoria and Albert print room, Townshend Bequest), no one may seriously start the freak collection. Notoriously, though, you never can be sure, and honesty bids me to say that any

THE PRINCE REGENT (GEO. IV.)

Shadow or negative silhouette to be held between light and paper.

xxxiv.

such collector will strike a rich lode in Smart of Frant, near Tonbridge Wells, who flourished around 1820. Smart as a young man started tailor, but soon he was an "Artist"; cutter—duly "to" a Royal Highness—of velvet-clothed and leather-gaitered people on a painted background, the whole adorned with spangles and backed by a printed poem wherein he compared himself naturally enough with Rubens, Aristotle, and some more of the best people.

There are many things even within the narrow radius of Shadow-art that nobody collects as yet. . .

Messieurs, faites vos jeux !

IX

"CUT PAPER"

CHAPTER IX

" CUT PAPER "

OUR judicial humorists at sundry recent times
have amused their public and gratified the Press by
long and comical debates on " What is a sardine ? "
and " What is swank ? " It is a pity that they did
not, so to speak, finish with the S's and proceed to
establish legally " What is a silhouette ? "

I have met both dealers and collectors who placed
under this elastic heading almost any side-face
portrait, whether in wax, brass, or wood. I have
equally met dealers and collectors who refused the
name silhouette to any portrait that had not a dead-
black face, ruling out Lea of Portsmouth or Foster
of Derby. They suffer, I imagine, from that little
knowledge which is so perilous, and fancy " silhouette " to be the French root-word for shadow.

Now, having met the information in line one of
every article upon the subject, I had made a vow
not to chronicle, unless allusively, the ancient fact
that the name Silhouette derived itself, in mockery

of meanness, from Etienne de Silhouette, French Minister of Finance in 1759. The art existed long before his time, and not till Edouart's day did the word "shade" or "profile" give place generally in England to the more ugly "silhouette." It therefore seems ridiculous to harp upon this accident of name. The derivation is, however, interesting because it seems to me that till the Courts decide, it is our best criterion. Silhouette, used as a word of scorn for everything cheap, fastened itself at last upon an art which only needed the simplest materials for its adequate fulfilment. Clearly, then, silhouette is not a term that can include such portraits as are modelled in wax or finely carved in wood. By its very origin, the word implies some effect gained with a rigid economy of means.

However ill-adapted, therefore, it may seem to the fine-worked gems of Mrs. Beetham, it surely fits with admirable exactness those delicious efforts to state landscape in the terms of paper, to which purists would deny the term. Groups such as Edouart's admittedly are silhouettes; add a tree or two and half a dozen cows—hey, presto! the thing has become "cut paper. . . ."! That is the theory; but though the last heading is convenient enough, I see

182

IN MEMORIAM, REBH. WOODS, DIED 1795.

Cut in blue paper and adorned with spangles.

no reason to regard cut paper as any more than just one kind of silhouette.

It is, in fact, a very interesting kind and one oddly neglected till of late by most collectors. Perhaps one reason is that it lacks documents or signatures to an unusual degree, so that, however much a man might become a connoisseur, he could not ever hope to be an expert. This is an undoubted drawback, for even a collector of beer-bottle corks finds some part of his joy in the glad consciousness that he knows All About Them.

Fancy designs were certainly cut by the professed silhouettists, as may be seen for instance from Gapp's label, but it is rare indeed that one finds a signed specimen of any early date; never (to dogmatize from only a fourteen-year search) one that bears a label. Abroad, it is true, the science would be easier, for Frederick Hendriks has recorded a visit at Dusseldorf to Wilhelm Müller, whose goats perched on abrupt hills one could recognize from the examples given; * there is Konewka whose illustrated edition of the *Midsummer's Night's Dream* is world famous; Mrs. Nevill Jackson records the names of Karl Fröhlich, Packeny of Vienna, Runge who cut flowers

* *The Queen*, Dec. 29, 1906.

that pleased Goethe ; whilst one of the most curious specimens in my collection—a crude and early " Crucifixion " surrounded by dice, scourges, ladders, the crowing cock, and all other emblems, finely cut in black—bears the cut inscription, " Verfertick L. Broc." In England, however, the would-be historian of cut-paper must wait, I think, until the day of Gapp or Hubard for his documents. The Hubard prodigy makes much play with cut paper in his elaborate advertisement and promises such varied fare as " Perspective Views, Architectural, Military, Sporting Pieces, Family Groups." It must (in the catchword of Master Hubard's age) be left to the ingenious reader to decide which heading covers the spirited design cut in blue paper by him that adorns plate xli. To me it suggests, more than anything, a crazy foreboding of the Russian ballet.

The fact is that this was a polite accomplishment ; taught—it would seem—in the seminaries for young ladies and afterwards practised in mere love by the Georgian damsel, who had no hockey or vote-meetings and could not always be enjoying the delirious excitement of having her shade taken. These elaborate designs of an astounding fineness may be the work of amateurs no less than the delicious needlework of the same period. It was, in fact, clearly the smart thing to do. Reference has been made in another chapter to the cut paper album of Lady Blessington, whilst in the Victoria and Albert Museum print-room may be found some classic and domestic scenes inscribed, " Copied by Mrs. Wigston from Lady Templetown's designs."

Sceptics, infused with the meaning of that poor submerged word " amateur " in this bridge-playing age, need only glance at pl. xxxv. Here, one would say, is work cut by a professional. The peacocks are of irreproachable design ; cupids and grapes alike are utterly beyond reproach ; the whole is beautifully cut in an effective dark blue paper. Silver and red adorn the coats-of-arms, as also the sexton and flight into Egypt, whilst the first colour gleams also from the latticed church window. Nothing could be finer, nothing more elaborate. Yet this is no more than a tribute to Rebeccah Woods by her heart-broken husband, for by the church-porch, underneath a weeping willow, there appears : "Reb$^{h.}$ Woods, Died 7 Sep$^{r.}$ 1795, Aged 37," and (always cut in the blue paper), these pathetic lines :

" Farewell, Dear Wife, thy lofs to us is great
Who is left behind to mourn thy last retreat.
A tender Wife and a Parent Dear
We Daily found in you while living here.
Her God hath cald her where She is shure to have
A Blifs more Solid than herSelf once gave."

Education has improved notoriously, since 1795, even among the educated classes ; but there are symptoms both in spelling and in grammar which hint that this beautiful specimen may be the work of a quite common man.

As to the manner of this handicraft, eye-witnesses agree that it was very swiftly done and—in its rougher forms—frequently with hands held under table. This, of course, was merely what we now call " swagger." Grannies and others who remember this talk with one consent of scissors : but there is little doubt that the fine earliest work—much of it done in the monasteries—was accomplished with a knife. Such incredible fineness could not be otherwise attained, and one specimen, of a saint with skull and cross reclining under trees, shows tiny birds disporting in a labyrinth of greenery that seems to leave no entry for the scissors. For those, however, who value half an ounce of fact more than two tons of logic there is proof in a later cutting of religious nature. An oddly compounded border of royal and religious emblems, cut in white, surrounds the Lord's Prayer and this poem of a simple charm :

> " 'Tis religion that can give
> Sweetest pleasures whilst we live.
> 'Tis Religion must supply
> Solid comfort when we die.
> After death its joys will be
> Lasting as eternity.
> Be living God our friend,
> Then our bliss shall Never end."

These lines conclude with a flower and " John Momfroy, 1831," whilst the prayer ends definitely, " Amen. Cut with a Knife." This rules out argument. . . .

It may, in fact, be said that the instrument used was a matter of caprice. Some curiously fine old cut-paper designs used to illustrate " The Sculptor Caught Napping " as recently as 1899 were produced by a combination of the methods. Jane E. Cook was the artist, and her descendant in a preface says : " To produce them white paper has been cut out with a pair of scissors, and the obvious necessity of adding essential details to the resulting outline was supplied by delicately marking the white paper with the fine point of a stiletto." A cameo-effect was thus obtained, and the designs make a fine contrast with plain black silhouettes that fill a corner of each page. Clearly this was the method used in a form of Victorian portrait-silhouette, where buttons, lace, creases, even hair and ear-rings, are pushed out in relief upon the black.

More doubt exists as to whether any form of magnifying spectacles was used, such as must surely have been employed by Miers and the others who did silhouettes for jewelled settings. If our dear grandmothers really cut these minute patterns without artificial aid, the process may explain our eyesight. Our grandparents have cut grapes and our children's eyes are set in spectacles. . . .

Mrs. Delany, indeed, whose name will always be associated with cut-paper work, did not begin this labour, which might seem to call for " young eyes," till she was amply seventy. She had, of course, long ere this given delight to George III, that enthusiastic amateur of all things odd, by her rolled-paper pictures, cardboard temples, and I know not

Plate XXXVI.

HERALDIC EMBLEM

Cut in white paper (xviii. century). Actual size.

what of curious enterprise ; but the inscription in her famous " Hortus Siccus," now in the British Museum, begins :

" Plants copied after Nature in paper Mosaick begun in the year 1774 :

> *Hail to the happy hour ! when Fancy led*
> *My pensive mind this flow'ry path to tread."*

A pæan of joy surprising when one reads :

" This paper mosaick work was first begun in the seventy-fourth year of my age (which I at first only meant as an imitation of an 'Hortus Siccus') as an employment and amusement, to supply the loss of those that had formerly been delightful to me ; but had lost their power of pleasing ; being deprived of that Friend, whose partial approbation, was my Pride, and had stamp't a value on them. . . ." (The reference is no doubt to her husband.)

This preface, which runs to some length, is signed " Mary Delany, Bulstrode, 5th July, 1779."

Three years later, or eight after the work's beginning, in a more shaky hand appears this tragic entry :

> " *The time is come.   I can no more*
> *The Vegetable world explore,*

No more with rapture cull each flower
That paints the mead or twines the Bower. . . .
Farewell to all those friendly Powers
That blest my solitary Hours.
Alas, farewell ! . . .
O ! sanctify the pointed Dart,
That at this Moment rends my Heart ;
Teach me submissive to resign
When summoned by thy Will Divine.

St. James Place, 1782.   M. D."

The flowers themselves, of which there are ten bulky volumes, are cut in small bits with no attempt at a bold sweep, and mounted upon black. Often the signature M. D. is cut out in black, and the specimens are dated. The colour is good and a fine effect is gained in such a specimen as that named " Lilium Canadensis " (this may be garden latin, so I leave it), with endless super-imposed reds, pinks, yellows, touched by spots of paint. On the whole, most success is gained with the small plants, for there is no pretence at grouping in the larger pieces ; but the realism of the work is startling, and it must always remain a wonderful achievement for so old a lady.

She did not at all events lack praise in her own day. "Letters from Mrs. Delany to Mrs. Frances Hamilton from the year 1779 to 1788," published by Longman in 1820 with a silhouette frontispiece of Mrs. Delany, is full of tributes from the greatest in the land. George III looked on the old lady as no less than a genius, and the kindness to her of him and his Queen seems to have had no limits. So late as 1787 Mrs. Preston writes, " The King and Queen . . . increase in affection and respect to Mrs. D., and the King always makes her lean on his arm. Her house is cheerful, and filled with her own charming works. No pictures have held their colours so well. I had time to look over near a volume of her flowers. She has finished nine hundred and eighty sheets, and regrets that the thousand she intended wants twenty of its full number." Dr. Darwin, author of the " Botanic Garden," wrote a poem beginning :

" *So now Delany forms her mimic powers,*
Her paper foliage and her silken flowers."

Whilst Mr. Gilpin, another author of those days, records in a book on the Highlands :
" In the progress of her work she pulls the flower in pieces—and having cut her papers to the shape

191

of the several parts, she puts them together, giving them a richness and consistence, by laying one piece over another, and often a transparent piece over part of a shade which softens it. Very rarely she gives any colour with a brush. . . . These flowers have both the beauty of painting and the exactness of botany; and the work, I have no doubt, into whatever hands it may hereafter fall, will be long considered as a great curiosity."

Finally, Mr. Chalmers in his Biographical Dictionary, having paid a tribute to her oil-paintings, embroidery, and shell-work, proceeds: " But what is more remarkable, at the age of seventy-four she invented a new and beautiful mode of exercising her ingenuity." The article is long, but as of chief interest emerge three facts: Mrs. Delany did not draw her flowers before she cut them—she dyed paper if none of the Chinese varieties at her disposal fitted Nature's hue—and by a pleasant touch which reveals the fine old lady (whom he calls "a noble ruin ") in a single human moment, he tells us that she would sometimes place a real leaf among her simulated ones and note with joy that nobody detected it. . . .

No greater mistake, however, could be made than

THE WHITE HOUSES

Cut with scissors by Mary Holland
before she was 10 years old, 1776.

to imagine that flowers or even landscapes exhausted
the resources of fancy-subject silhouette. Its variety
indeed would be not the least charm for a collector ;
and it may be at once asserted with dogmatic brevity
(for a whole book could easily be written on so-called
" cut-paper ") that in this department of silhouette
one can not speak of any decadence. These fancy-
cuts had always something childish in them—whence
their perennial attraction. They were a thing that
people did " for fun " ; and often enough that is
how the things most worth while are produced.
How proud these craftsmen were as their original
conception grew, how hard it was to lay the master-
piece aside or make the dull admission that it had
been finished ! Of course they did not ! No, they
added spangles. . . . There was never any classic
severity about cut-paper, and so it follows there can
be no decadence. True, one of the earliest specimens
in my tentative collection, undated but marked
Jacobean by its frame and spirit, shows the simplicity of old lace in its fine design ; but one no later
has all the glory of straw buildings, multicoloured
peacocks, and silk-garbed courtiers.

Children with stiff arms averted from their take-
off clothes ; birds that gain colour (through slit

paper) from silk gummed below ; paper in varied thicknesses, to show sunsets and varied light-effects when held up to a candle ; handsomely clothed figures before cut and painted backgrounds ; elaborate Dutch landscapes, whole avenues of wobbly cut-out trees, encased in deep, worm-eaten boxes ; a pair of urns with gorgeous bouquets of lavishly protruding blossoms, one inscribed " Julia," the other " Kate " ; cut-paper fans ; a candle-screen, cut flowers between talc ; Napoleon profile in black with every fold of his coat shown, the high lights got by the white paper background ; the same front-face, an awful and quite un-Imperial sight ; a troop of cavalry, showing their black shadows cast before them by an equally black sun ; monkish productions, the work of hands left idle by the printing-press and its swift victory over manuscript—productions often not far from that kindred hobby, pin-prick pictures ; early sporting scenes, cut in white paper or (a later luxury) in gold, with dogs that pounce at abrupt angles upon hinds or hares quite undismayed ; delicious imitations of worked samplers, with crazy houses in the background and before them a post-impressionist menagerie of animals in sizes never planned by nature, vast swans swimming past wee stepping horses or timid ladies overshadowed by well-nourished swine : without discussing such old circles as are found in watches or square end-papers seen in ancient tomes, what end should there be to enumerating the varieties of subject-silhouette ?

One or two only must have fuller mention, and for varied reasons.

There are people who, under a pretence of system, revel in dividing everything under so many headings that the result is a glorious confusion. These have invented the weird term " Lace-paper." The work which it is meant to cover is nothing more than paper so finely cut that it resembles lace. The effect is naturally more striking in such a specimen as I have mentioned, the early design copied almost certainly from a lace model : but no less delightful when the imitation or pretence is cast totally aside. One, something of a compromise, shows a border clearly modelled upon lace, in its appropriate white, though in the centre is a delicately painted oval emblem—tambourine, flute, music, roses, doves—an utterly harmonious decoration set against black silk and shrined in its deep oval frame made by a carver at " No. 2, the East End of Middle Row, Holborn Bars." Other specimens of the same period, late

eighteenth century, abandon more entirely the
pretence of lace, for though of even more astounding
fineness, their inspiration is from heraldry. The late
Lady Dorothy Nevill, one of the first connoisseurs
in this cut-paper, had a fine specimen of this work,
mounted on a mirror. One in my collection shows
the Beauchamp-Procter arms : namely (so a herald
tells me), " Quarterly I. and IV. ; Argent, a
Chevron between three martlets sable—Procter II.
and III. ; Gules, a fess, between six billets (three
and three barways), or ; a canton ermine—Beau-
champ. Crest : On a mount vert, a grey hound
sejant argent, spotted brown, collared or. Motto :
Toujours fidèle." I can at least guarantee the
motto, and hope the rest is copied out correctly. . . .
The whole, which I should have called a wolf and
greyhound each side of a coat-of-arms enclosed in a
garter bearing the words " Tria Juncta In Uno," is
in white paper, marvellously cut down to the tiniest
rose, crown, or thistle. It is pressed between two
bits of glass and then enclosed in a fine carved black
and gilt frame, which carries Christie's mark. A
circular specimen, even more minute, shows two
cupids holding up a hatchment with three lions on it,
(this is not the herald's wording). They perch upon

a cloud and all around them are flowers or emblems of an incredible minuteness. The motto in this case is " La Vertu et la Sagesse Conduisent au Bonheur." This is cut in white and laid on blue, except that the hatchment bears a fittingly black background. Over it one of the cupids holds a wreath enclosing the initials " J. C. E." Inspection of this specimen, which only measures exactly four inches across leaves one incredulous—till one reflects that even nowadays machines are left lagging far behind, when it comes to the finer arts. Photography, in fact, jibs oddly at these tiny cuttings and this one can only be shown with much of its fine detail lost (pl. xxxvi).

One need not wonder that Reproduction jibs at another of my pet specimens, for this is eighteen inches by a foot and even the original is packed with detail. The scheme is indeed ambitious. The thing might be said to hold almost All Life in its futuristic borders—at any rate, the whole life of a household. The hour is five to eight, so much one sees from the kitchen clock, and one may safely add A.M. Madam, on the top floor is a-bed, but yet so much awake that baby has been brought to her. Her boots are ready, too, beneath the dressing-table ; the kettle boils, and pussy seems to point at something edible.

Breakfast in bed, perhaps ? Those labelled bottles on the mantelpiece half hint at sickness, till with a real relief we see that Madam's hat and parasol are hung up ready for the afternoon. Besides, no invalid could bear those statues in her room. . . . Down in the drawing-room, where flowers luxuriate and the best china lives, it is a scene of opulence. The pictures are by Masters clearly ; silhouettes flank the mirror (of a silver tinsel) ; a red tinsel fire blazes extravagantly behind a fender of pure gold. The carpet, as upstairs, has a green ground ; a colour shared by one of the two birds. The husband—or son ?—is alert already. Quill in hand he balances himself grimly on one of the crazy-angled chairs and reaps the morning hour. Man must work, though woman may sleep ! Gran'pa—surely it can't be the husband—is less philosophic. He has reached the age when Man may keep his hat on, and he is querulous. Even nicotine does not console him. " Dang these chairs," you can hear him complain. . . The lowest floor is more compendious, for here we get the garden too. Alas, dark doings are afoot so early. Well may the parrot or peacock look stiffly surprised, well may Fido bark and snarl beneath the drying clothes, for I regret to say the daughter of the house (note her smart crinoline), is meeting with a common soldier, oddly 1790. Meanwhile, in the kitchen, birds break in and steal the pudding, whilst yet another dog (or it may be a rat) barks up at them from underneath the table. Next comes the servant's bedroom where of course—for this is 1830, by the daughter's dress—the best furniture is kept ; the scullery with yet another swain attendant ; and last of all, beneath a gamp suspended in mid-air, there mounts the parlour-maid with tea (we now perceive it all) for Madam. The first five steps alone are seen —but the last four emerge in Madam's room. . . . Who after this shall say the past too did not have its futurists ?

This perfect microcosm, cut in black, is headed by an allegoric group, beautifully wrought but of a meaning far beyond me. I seem dimly to discern a cupid and a Juno, but she may be Venus. . . . A rather naturally dubious-looking angel ends the riotous procession.

Here is the whole preposterous, delightful, art of subject-silhouette at its high-water mark, and those who do not like it must collect Staffordshire or postage stamps. They have not the cut-paper mind. . . .

THE ART OF SILHOUETTE

Of course there are simpler designs for those who have the classic bent. The beautiful white houses joined by bridges (pl. xxxvii) are beyond reproach as a design, and not a spangle anywhere upon them: although the work of childish hands. " Cut with scissors by Miss Mary Holland, Born on the Pedlar's Acre March 7, 1770, before she was ten years old," runs the inscription, proudly attested by " Mrs. Mary Ann Davis, Senior." From another specimen, largely similar but with a less successful border, we learn that Mrs. Davis was Mary's mother-in-law at a later date. Then there is, not signed unluckily or dated save by its poke-bonnets, a delicious pier with cut-paper waves and an idle crowd of sight-seers; or white birds on black backgrounds, with wings cut in relief—a refinement found so early as 1757. Sometimes, even, the art of painting was put under contribution for a subject, and opposite may be found an adaptation of Morland's famous picnic. Paper and style alike proclaim this an eighteenth century piece, and it is of interest to note that the silhouettist, so early, has not boggled at one full-face figure. It cannot be claimed that this is an improvement on the old convention : but in a signed portrait of an officer by Torond a pleasant effect is gained by

THE ANGLERS' REPAST, after Morland.

Cut in black paper (xviii century).   Size of original 19-in. × 16.

the black profile placed over a body painted (as it were !) full face in grey, brown, and black.

And lastly, lest to close upon these plain specimens should kindle heresies on decadence, a specimen no later shows a full-face Ceres walking through the corn whilst cupids riot round her and a dragon looking very out of place lies by her side. Lutes, drums, scrolls of music, mix with birds and squirrels in the splendidly cut border and no colour almost in the rainbow is found wanting.

In short, for once embarked upon cut-paper, I grow tedious, here ready for collectors is a field whose great charm is the unexpected. You never may become an expert . . . but you can never grow accustomed. Each specimen shows something new.

Lately, in the provinces, a dealer in reply to my inquiries said : " Now what a pity, sir, you didn't call in a few days ago. I had a table covered with that queer old stuff. Oh, it *was* finely cut. I never saw such work ; but no one seemed to fancy it, and so I scraped it off. A fine old Chippendale piece it was too. I wish I'd known you cared for that old paper-work. . . ."

We all have our tragedies. And I console myself with the reflection that it may have happened twenty years ago, or even not at all.   Certainly no seasoned connoisseur will vex his soul about the old old tale : " I've just sold such a beauty."   These are the lures of a dealer who wishes one to call again ; arts no less obvious than those of the dear, simple collector who believes in the policy of " stalking-horses."   Averting his eye doggedly from the object he is panting to possess, he asks in hang-dog tones, " Have you got any miniatures of Nelson ? " or something similar. The dealer scarcely worries to reply.   To him this is a query in the class of " How d'you do ? "   To answer in full betrays social inexperience.   " No, sir," he says tolerantly : " do you collect anything else ? "   " Well," answers the wily one, striving to combine a calm voice with his bumpy heart, " what's that old black portrait on chalk—is it ? —in the window ? " . . .   The dealer turns his back to get it, and his smile is hidden.   Another silhouette collector !

Ye gods, what fools we mortals be !   But it is of such harmless comedies that is compounded the pleasant friendship between dealer and collector ; a genial freemasonry that possibly no other trade can show.

X
PRACTICAL

CHAPTER X

PRACTICAL

THIS is a sordid chapter. People with beautiful white souls had better pass on to the next.

Most of us, however, deep down in our hidden selves, have a black spot which hankers to worst some one in a deal, or—at the very nicest—never to be worsted by another. Even those who begin to spell art with a big A usually let £ *s. d.* creep into it before the end.

I had intended maxims for collectors, and in my earlier note-books I find a few jotted down.

" *Buy at the cheapest and sell at the dearest shop.*
What's broken can't be mended, however well restored.
Look at the silhouette, mistrust the signature behind.
Never think anyone ignorant except yourself."

What excellent good sense, and how entirely useless ! Splendid faith of Youth, which had planned counsel no less wasted than the mumbled saws of grandpapa, that fall upon the deaf ears of Inexperience, longing indeed to be wise but thinking error the pathway of more promise. What is the use of knowledge learnt by others ? Find it yourself, it is a pearl beyond all price ; let anyone else offer it, the thing is boring rubbish. . . .

And yet there may be some few anxious to know what to buy, where to find it, and what to avoid.

As to the last, a fascinating subject, the dangers are not yet so great as they will be in the near future. Even forgers stand in need of education and so far I have seen few of them advanced beyond the idea of silhouette as a cut-paper portrait. London of late has been deluged with a series of six heads. Every framemaker and most antique-dealers have been victimized by these rough cuttings, all bearing pencilled names of such high sound as Cromwell and Napoleon. Some one has been busy with his scissors ! Diverging here, I may embark on yet another maxim. Always be suspicious of silhouettes purporting to be Nelson or men of an equal name. They may of course be ancient, they almost certainly will not be Nelson, who was much busier than George III. The placing of great names on unidentified old silhouettes is quite a hobby with some dealers, and, I may add, with some collectors also. Turning to those that are not old there is one series of fakes not cut out of paper but done upon flat glass. Some of these are ladies—Antoinette, one may be sure—but most of them are Generals or Admirals of old-world repute. The names of these are written on the glass (a thing I can recall in no authentic specimen), usually with one letter above another, like the signature of a Japanese print or forged wax medallion. Anyone with half an ounce of observation can detect these from the fact that the glass is too big and the ink of a dirty unconvincing brown. Equally unsatisfying to anyone not fatally myopic is the attempt to gild the cut-out shadow. Where the difference lies it is not easy to describe in words, but colour and above all *touch* are wrong. The most frequent gilt specimen that I have seen is of a youth, rather large in size, inscribed with the fine name " Sir Rainald Knightley." This may be found in plain black also or on a curious pink glass. Dear Sir Rainald, he is an old friend. I have met him in a score of shops and half as many guises. He must be, in popularity, a close rival to George Washington.

Quite an interesting collection might be made of fakes, and indeed Mrs. Nevill Jackson told me once that she intended it. Another could be formed,

cheerily amusing, of the poor unknown folk who
have been posthumously christened Wellington,
Queen Charlotte, Washington, or Marie Antoinette.
I have a really fine old silhouette of a young man in the
eighteen-twentys inscribed Napoleon, and once possessed a duly autographed Dickens, superb in college
cap :—what irony to those who know his younger days !

Frames are no guide, even when you have learnt
to know at sight those brought into being through
wholesale massacre of papier mâché trays and
fitted with thin acorns of new brass. They are a
snare, indeed, for many an old frame has held a
silhouette cut from the *Connoisseur* and backed by
a reprint of the 1810 *Observer* or sections from old
calf book-bindings, whilst that delicious lady in
the top-hat from Mrs. Nevill Jackson's book must
be quite used, by now, to an old thin brass oval ! She
certainly is charming as a decoration, but I have met
her in some good collections. These are the moments
when tact fights with truth. I have also, in my wander-
ings, met many a gilt silhouette ascribed to Edouart,
clearly by people who have never read that stern
profilist's warm comments on this " unnatural "
addition to the shadow proper. Edouart, by the
way, although commonly called Auguste, signed

" Aug^n· Edouart," short for Augustin, a curious fact ignored by one forger whose clever work has come my way.

Well, they will learn, as they have learnt in needle-work and china. Soon we shall have them working upon chalk like Miers, rivalling the daintiness of Mrs. Beetham, and then the real fun will begin, for what else is Collecting than a contest of wits, a trial of strength, one more form of all-inclusive sport ? Soon, too, no doubt we shall have beautiful cut-papers and they will be ashamed of the one specimen that I have so far seen, though I have seen it often : Victoria, crudely cut, with wobbly generals reviewing the troops at her coronation.

What to buy, then, these ignored ?

First of all, of course—if you can—specimens on chalk or glass, complete in pear-wood or brass oval, with label still unbroken, and the beautiful old convex glass adorned with patterns in the gold and white. Here is the cream of silhouette and I will allow counterfeiters a good century before they reach to it. But even when fate does not smile to this extent, one often finds labelled specimens, and these should be preferred for reasons clear from the pages before this. Eighteenth-century portraits, too, are an obvious objective, and plain black profiles, or black and grey—contrary to vulgar prejudice— are better than the gilt, unless these last are labelled Miers.

After a little, naturally, collectors will learn the styles of profilists so surely that the author of a profile can be named at sight. For this, like all else, there is no master but experience. All of the great exponents had tricks of their own, as I have tried to show in chapter iii, and by these their work may be recognized without the possibility of error. Lately, in visiting Mr. Wellesley's collection, I was able to identify two specimens in mine, entirely individual but unluckily not signed. In one case, it was a fine portrait of an officer, painted on glass to throw the shadow on to chalk behind ; the body as dark as in work by Charles, the face curiously transparent. In Mr. Wellesley's collection I found one done in exactly the same formula and signed by Lea of Portsmouth, who no doubt mostly painted martial sitters. The other specimen was yet more individual, not so much from its style of paint as from the method of its setting. Here (for it was in fact a pair) portraits delicately painted on flat glass were surrounded by an oval of holes pierced in the black,

AN OFFICER

By H. P. Roberts, painted on flat glass.

thus displaying circles of a gold-leaf laid behind. This novel method of obtaining a gold-and-black border was, I now learn, the speciality of H. P. Roberts. As this artist signed but little, yet did work easy to recognize at sight, I reproduce the specimen, pl. xxxix. At Knole there is a pair by H. P. Roberts upon which I could find no name, and other connoisseurs or owners may be helped to a sure attribution

Upon the point of what to buy it would be idle to say more. The best, naturally : and the gift to recognize it is a gift from heaven. There is in good things, as old Plato knew, an intrinsic quality, unmistakable and indescribable, so that a man who has once learnt the meaning of the Good will know instinctively good china, good prints, good silhouettes, good anything at all. The tragedy of this world is that most people have a flair only for the bad. . . .

Some portraits simply cut-out are of value, others would be dear at threepence ; with which obvious but deep remark, and the advice that broken specimens are never cheap, I must pass on to my next heading, " Where To Buy."

London, certainly. Ask any dealer, he will say the same. So far as antiques go, it is indeed " the

market of the world." The Paris quays ? Paris is
buying old stuff (*and* new) daily from the London
dealers. In Germany, as France, the silhouette
has won its way back earlier than here, and everything is snapped up for that market from the London
shops.

London is the place, but use a little common sense.
Think of the rents, and buy where the big dealers
buy. Not in draughty cattle markets, exploited
by reporters and stocked largely by the West-end
brokers, but in the little back-streets and the outer
suburbs. Yet equally, since any dogma holds about
as much truth as its opposite, often a big dealer will
scornfully ask nothing for small things bought in a
lot with something that he wanted.

Least satisfactory of all must be accounted private
bargains. The man who knows nothing about
values does not favour anyone except himself. He
has " been told that it is very valuable." It certainly
is " very old." He would not sell if he did not
want money instantly. He thinks it should be
worth a five-pound note to you. And a remittance
will oblige. . . .

Lately, a Yorkshire worthy wrote to me, saying
he had two silhouettes " on paper, framed in ebony,"

and—alternate formula—desired an offer. A friend had "made an offer for them and said they were valuable." Admiring the superior honesty of a friend who apparently in one breath could make these two remarks, I answered that I could perhaps do more if I might either see the silhouettes or else know what his friend had offered. This last altogether without guile:—I wished to see what was expected of me. Perhaps I never quite realized what havoc ten years of London had played with my moral sense till I received his answer. I was to understand that it would not be fair to his friend to give his bid away; "folks in Yorks," did *not* transact business in that way. The silhouettes were marvellously "well preserved," and had "always been displayed in his drawing-room"; and when he was next in London he would "call into Christie's with them and have them valued properly." . . .

Dear me, what a lot of life's fun is missed by those poor people who are not collectors!

XI

NOW—
AND WHAT THEN?

CHAPTER XI

NOW—AND WHAT THEN?

IT is an amusing modern affectation to look down on all the old accomplishments, as one who should say : " Poor dears, and so they really did these things ? How bored they must have been. Imagine never having to extend your mind as you must do at Bridge ! " . . . .

Thus a lover of the eighteenth-century profiles, hearing much chatter as to Silhouette's revival, naturally looks for big things indeed. He looks for these condescending moderns to improve upon the old accomplishment they have revived. . . .

He may look.

Let me not be thought to say a word against the many profilists who have sprung up, by the old law of demand, like mystic mushrooms upon every side. Monsieur Bly, of the West Pier at Brighton, is probably the best known among those who have been established long before the new revival. He cuts free hand, with fine contempt for the preliminary

217

sketch, but owns an open mind, for whilst a warm
defender of the Edouart convention, he is an experimentalist, as all self-respecting silhouettists should
be. His fancy cuts have long shared the reputation
of his portraits, and he is now embarking on a
variant of the old black-and-gold glass etching.

Handrup, established at the Crystal Palace, who
cuts out fine portraits in two minutes, equally shows
a pretty taste for fancy-subjects ; a department,
however, in which the name of Captain Tharpe must
stand supreme among the living silhouettists. Baron
Scotford has lately come to Regent Street,—via
Paris, Rome, Brussels, and Glasgow,—from America,
nor need those who know anything of Silhouette
marvel that a land reputed modern should give
out such old-world products, for was she not the
home of Peale and Patience Wright ? did she not
welcome to her bosom Edouart and Master Hubard ?

Scotford in any case is an accomplished and a rapid
cutter. Setting his patron against a light background, but with no intervening screen, he draws
a rough outline in pencil (a habit deprecated, be it
said, by Handrup no less than by Bly), and doubling
a piece of thin black paper snips it with astounding
sureness as he turns it hither and thither in a

MICKIEWICZ, POLISH POET

Painted on card by Phil May, 1888.

xl.

bewildering way. It may be here remarked that Bly, whilst commonly working in a like manner, sometimes uses an adaptation of the " camera lucida," a pleasant contrivance by which one finds the sitter's head placed at a convenient size upon the paper laid before one. This is of interest as showing a recurrence to the old advertised " machine."

The whole of this modern paper-cutting is in fact full of an interest, however melancholy, to lovers of the old. Scotford is of Edouart's school, but whilst he has a happy gift for faces, especially of children, he lacks his predecessor's odd sense of the character in clothes. A portrait, for instance, of George Grossmith Junior, individual and able, carries the line from chest to knee in a pure curve, artistically good perhaps—for Scotford wielded the brush in Paris ateliers before he grasped the scissors—but surely not sartorially true. Edouart could show a man's soul in his buttons !

In any case, I repeat, there is no word to be said against these cut-portraits, but they do not seem quite enough to justify the big word, " revival." In the best days of Silhouette, this book has shown, the finest artists never touched a pair of scissors. As to this, Scotford confessed to me that he had never seen a Miers, Rosenberg or Beetham, whilst Handrup in an interesting booklet makes the rather astonishing assertion: "In days gone by . . . a few painted exquisitely on ivory and plaster with or without gold ; some on glass, china, silk or paper ; others used mechanical devices, but it was considered the proper and most artistic way to cut with scissors direct from black paper . . . without any drawing or outlining beforehand. This of course was very difficult, but on the other hand they were able to obtain better results, because if a line be drawn ever so fine sharp scissors will cut it finer, even a hair's thickness too much or too little altering the whole expression —it is here the art of the executor lies."

"It was considered. . . ." Here indeed is Edouart redivivus! In fact, this whole "revival" is oddly like Edouart's "renaissance." In neither case is anything at all heard of those great eighteenth-century artists who made Silhouette an art to be compared in its fineness and decorative charm with that of miniature.

But even if it were, even if our reigning beauties could still pay down their guineas to have their noses immortalized on plaster, are there not already enough arts content to rest weakly on bad copies of great achievements in the years gone by ? Will no man of creative, of inventive force, a second Foster, throw in his lot with this poor dainty art, crushed out of sight for half a century by the banausic camera and just beginning to crawl back ? Phil May has shown a little how modern formulæ could be adapted to this old-world art, and years ago in Edgware Road I had the good luck to find three delicious painted specimens, of which one may be seen upon pl. xl. Signed " Phil May, '88, Paris, Chat Noir," it is a portrait of Mickiewicz, the Polish Poet. Paganini—so Edouart tells us with pride—was wont to declare that Edouart's portrait was the only one which did not burlesque him. I am ready to wager about Mickiewicz, " though I have never seen him " (to use the ingenuous Lavater's favourite formula), that no artist using any other method could convey to the spectator a more vivid, a more genially illuminating impression of the man in his habit as he lived than poor Phil May has given in this brilliant profile. The other two, representing the artist himself with his perpetual cigar and Kennedy of the old Aquarium instinct with the showman's suave assurance, are portraits just as firmly satisfying ; rousing sad regrets but also encouraging the hope that some fine artist may yet turn his gifts to portrait silhouette in some sense broader than the snipped-out paper.

Meanwhile, Silhouette is King—after his fashion. . . .

Every one suddenly is a collector of the antique shadows.   Dealers who, asked for them five years ago, sniffed " We don't worry about them," are now canvassing the lucky buyers.   Museums, imprudently void of silhouettes till now, are hastily buying before the market rises further, and already Walter Scott, Liston (two portraits, one the duplicate of that upon pl. xix), and other of the new-found Edouarts are in the National Portrait Gallery, whilst many more have gone to Edinburgh and Dublin.   Photographers, quick to embrace the rival they had thought long dead, are imitating the cut-paper by taking portraits close against a light-backed screen.   The daily Press begins to call woman's latest modish shape her silhouette. Black tardily becomes a fashionable colour ; cushions, curtains, posters, everywhere is the reaction to Simplicity. Sumurun's shadow-frieze set the stage-managers wide-eyed and minarets are everywhere against the sky. The music halls are never far behind. " The Shadow Man and Lady Silhouette :   Artistic, Amusing, and Always

Cut (1) by Master Hubard and (2) by Edouart (1826.)

Successful," " Silveno's Gallantygraph from U.S.A.,
embracing hand shadows, silhouettes, and mechanical
figures, ships, &c."—these from a recent Organ of
Variety ! Artists without the e are quickly falling
to the subject-silhouette, however shy as yet of
portraiture Maxwell Ayrton has produced some
utterly delightful coaching-scenes,—drawn of course,
not cut,—and by his kindness I am able to use one as
this book's end-papers. This is a thoroughly successful adaptation of the cut-paper formula to Painting,
and Arthur Rackham also has used it, with a sure
art no less than Konewka's, in his recent decorations
for " Æsop's Fables." The humorists of course
have long since seen its inimitable worth. Leslie
Willson, in the cycling days, did a whole book-full
called, " The Scorcher's Progress," wherein a red-
profile cyclist pursues his path through dead-black
traffic of assorted kinds, routing even the Life Guards
before a light yellow St. James's Palace, until at last
he meets with a steam-roller. This is a thoroughly
clever English specimen of modern silhouette, well
able to hold its own with the attempts of Caran
d'Ache. More recently, our comic artists have used
the method freely ; men of standing like Charles
Pears, or that most luxuriant of grotesque draughts-

men, H. M. Bateman, who has perpetrated some delirious shadows.

Perhaps, in fact, the use of Silhouette in humour may largely claim to be a modern product, although invented long before the so-called great revival, which cannot snatch this credit as its own.

Well, it is young, and meanwhile, turning away from the half-crown cut-out, however excellent; looking up for hope and consolation to the dainty old-world portraits gleaming on our walls; those of us who love poor Silhouette and know what he has been, rejoice to see him raised by the fickle crowd on to his throne again, even if he be but a shade of his own shadowy self.

FINIS

INDEX

AMELIA, Princess, 125

BRITISH Museum, 91

CHALMERS, 192
Christie, 196
COLLECTORS :
    Brown, Rev. Forster, 85
    Cairnes, Mrs., 59
    Dorotti, Madame, 84
    Fleming, Mrs., 66
    Guest, Montague, 72, 168
    Jackson, Mrs. Nevill, 11, 13, 14, 32, 57, 66,
        103, 117, 118, 145, 207, 208
    Lane, John, 72
    Nevill, Lady Dorothy, 125, 175, 196
    Sackville, Lady, 14, 56, 159–162
    Snow, Major-General D'Oyly, 116
    Stanton, Captain, 60
    Talbot, Hon. Miss Frances, 126
    Taylor, Mrs. Bromley, 163, 164
    Tweedie, Mrs. Alec, 113
    Weguelin, Mrs., 72
    Wellesley, Mr. Francis, 14, 31, 52, 66, 67, 71,
        72, 74, 110, 113, 114, 125, 143, 165–169, 210
    Wyatt, Mrs., 110, 113, 114
Connor, Mr., 107

DARWIN, Dr., 191
Davis, Mrs. Mary Ann, senr., 200
Downman, 167

P

INDEX

GILPIN, Mr., 191

HAMILTON, Mrs. Frances, 191

KNOLE, 36, 56, 159, 167, 211

LACE-PAPER, 195
Lavater, J. G., 33–35, 41–44, 97, 125, 172, 173, 221
Lucas, 163
Lukis, Frederica, 104, 116, 117

McRAE, John, 150
Mills, Weymer, 54, 169

NATIONAL Portrait Gallery, 31, 222

RUSKIN, John, 34

SILHOUETTE, Etienne de, 12, 182
SILHOUETTISTS :
    Adolphe, 114, 122
    Atkinson, G., 31
    Ayrton, Maxwell, 223
    Bateman, H. M., 224
    Beaumont, 83, 92, 116, 126, 170
    Beetham, Mrs., 13, 30, 37, 38, 45, 47–50, 54, 61,
        62, 65, 66, 72, 86, 89, 109, 124, 137–141, 160,
        166, 168, 170, 182, 209, 220
    Belluti, 174
    Blessington, Countess of, 127, 185
    Bly, Monsieur, 217–219
    Broc, Verfertick L., 184
    Bull, Mrs., 51
    Charles, 13, 22, 49–51, 54, 62, 85, 89, 146, 170,
        210
    Coog, 161
    Cook, Jane E., 187
    d'Ache, Caran, 223
    Dashwood, Lady, 125

INDEX

SILHOUETTISTS—*continued*

Delaney, Mrs., as subject, 31 ; as cut-paper artist, 188–192

Dempsey, 154

Driscoll, 116

Edouart, Augustin Amant Constance Fidèle, 12, 13, 29, 32, 37, 46, 54, 63, 80, 83, 97–112, 116–118, 147–151, 160, 170, 172, 173, 182, 208, 209, 218–221

Field, 63, 75, 76, 145, 146, 168, 170

Foster, of Derby, 56–61, 64, 81, 82, 92, 121, 161, 164, 170, 181, 221

Frith, F., 75, 77, 78, 92, 170

Frohlich, Karl, 183

Gapp, J., 46, 80, 154, 183, 184

Gonord, 113

Haines, 136, 154

Hamlet, 66, 170

Handrup, 218, 220

Harrington, Mrs., 71

Hervé, 63, 75–77, 170

Holland, Miss Mary, 200

Hubard, Master, 31, 32, 78, 79, 136, 151–153, 170, 184, 218

Hunt, Mrs. Leigh, 31, 32, 124

Jorden, 52, 66, 170

Joubert, 161

Kelfe, Lane, 124

Kennedy, 221

Konewka, 172, 183, 223

Lea, of Portsmouth, 181, 210

Lightfoot, Mrs., 143

Lovell, Thomas, 145

MacKenzie, Laura, 126

May, Phil, 221

Miers, John, 13, 30, 32, 45, 61–66, 72, 76, 82, 92, 109, 118, 136, 142–147, 160, 164, 166, 168, 170, 171, 188, 209, 220

INDEX

SILHOUETTISTS—*continued*

    Mitchell, J. S., 60, 61

    Momfroy, John, 187

    Müller, Wilhelm, 160, 183

    Packeny, 183

    Peale, 218

    Pears, Charles, 223

    Phelps, 74

    Phillp, John, 124

    Prosopographus, 88, 89

    Pye, John, 163

    Rackham, Arthur, 223

    Roberts, H. P., 211

    Rosenberg, Charles, 30, 37, 43, 45, 48, 51–54, 89, 107, 136, 141, 142, 151, 160, 167, 168, 170, 172, 220

    Rosier, James, junr., 80

    Rought, 73, 147

    Rudolph, 175

    Runge, 183

    Schatzmann, 125

    Scotford, Baron, 218, 219

    Seville, F. W., 91

    Skeolan, 154

    Spornberg, W., 54–57, 82, 161, 168, 170

    Templeton, Lady, 185

    Tharp, Captain, 218

    Thomason, I., 147, 170

    Torond, 71, 107, 113, 147, 200

    Tussaud, J. P., 88

    Wellings, 161

    Wigston, Mrs., 185

    Willson, Leslie, 223

    Woodham, J., 86

    Woods, 185

    Wright, Mrs. Patience, 113, 218

    Young, W. M., 84

Smith, Albert, 172

INDEX

Stadler, 172
Subject-silhouettes, 183–201
SUBJECTS :
  Alexandra, Queen, 160
  Ansley family, 56
  Awdry, the Misses, 83
  Bedford, Duchess of, 160
  Brougham, Lord, 171
  Browning, Robert, 32
  Buckland, Dr., 102
  Burney family, 110
  Burney, Fanny, 32
  Burns, Mrs., 143
  Burns, Robert, 32, 171
  Byron, Lord, 32
  Charles X, 32, 101
  Charlotte, Queen, 31, 163
  Dalrymple, Sir Hew, 72
  Darling, daughters of Sir Ralph, 117
  Derby, Countess of, 160
  D'Oyly, Sir Thomas, 116
  Egerton, Mrs., 176
  Elizabeth, Princess, 31 ; as amateur artist, 124, 125, 176
  Erskine, 176
  Fauconberg, Lord, 161
  Frederick of Prussia, 173
  Fisher, Kitty, 176
  Fitzherbert, Mrs., 31
  Fox, Charles James, 31
  George III, 31, 60, 72, 162, 163, 167, 171–173, 188, 191
  George IV, 31, 52, 176
  Gibbon, Edward, 31, 171
  Goethe, 31, 167 ; as amateur profilist, 113
  Goldsmith, Oliver, 31
  Grey, Earl, 171
  Grossmith, George, junr., 219

229

INDEX

SUBJECTS—*continued*

Gutch, Rev. John, 103
Harrison, General, 73
Howe, Lord (reputed), 63
Johnstone, Mrs., 176
Jones, Miss Di, 47, 49
Josephine, Empress, 164
Kean, Edmund, 176
Keate, Dr., 171
Keats, John, 32
Keith, Sir Robert, 72
Knightley, Sir Rainald, 207
Lee, James, 152
Liston, John, 108, 222
Magendie, Bishop of Bangor, 98
Massy, Hon. C., 146
Mathews, Mrs., 47, 49
Mickiewicz, 221
Napoleon, 31, 164
Nelson, Lord, 31, 85
O'Connell, Daniel, 171
Paganini, 32, 221
Parry family, 126
Pembroke, Earl of, 72
Pitt, William, 31, 92, 174
Pius VI, Pope, 57–59
Pompadour, Mme. de, 32
Robinson, Perdita, 31
Russell, Lord John, 171
Sackville, Lord, 160
Scott, Sir Walter, 32, 66, 222
Siddons, Mrs., 176
Simeon, Dr., 109, 151
Smart, 168
Stephens, Miss, 176
Symons, Benjamin Parsons, 103
Thomson, David, 129–132
Thun (? Thier), Mdlle., 72, 73

INDEX

SUBJECTS—*continued*
    Tyler, President John, 103
    Victoria, Queen, 31
    Wellington, Duke of, 32, 77, 85
    William IV, 31
    White, Blanco, 103
Swift, Jonathan, 46

TOMKINS, 125
Townshend, Barbara Anne, 172
Tuer, Andrew, 33

VICTORIA and Albert Museum, 33, 166, 170, 176, 185

PRINTED BY
BALLANTYNE & COMPANY LTD
LONDON

95